29.95

WRITING THE WORLD

Understanding William Stafford

WRITING THE WORLD

Understanding William Stafford

Judith Kitchen

Oregon State University Press
Corvallis

The paper in this book meets the guidelines for permanence and durability of the Committee on Production Guidelines for Book Longevity of the Council on Library Resources and the minimum requirements of the American National Standard for Permanence of Paper for Printed Library Materials Z39.48-1984.

Library of Congress Cataloging-in-Publication Data
Writing the world / understanding William Stafford / Judith Kitchen
  p. cm.
Includes bibliographical references and index.
ISBN 0-87071-456-2 (alk.)
1. Stafford, William, 1914-1993—Criticism and interpretation.
I Title.
PS3537.T143Z74 1999
811'.54—dc21   98-40553
                                               CIP

Oregon State University Press
101 Waldo Hall
Corvallis OR 97331-6407
541-737-3166 •fax 541-737-3170
www.osu.orst.edu/dept/press

Contents

Introduction

The writer and critic Fred Chappell once suggested that, for Stafford, the word *world* was a trope for *loss*,[1] but in one of his later poems Stafford seemed to equate the world with something waiting to be found:

Writing the World

In the stillness around me that no one can cross
I am writing for life.
The world like a leaf turns as it falls.
This air might catch, an edge touch
that leaf, and a song begin till
all turns red.
I can feel that song by holding my hand
on a picture of fire, saying, "Burn"—

That kind of world. There is
fire and you say so—your tongue takes
flame. You burn into speech.
You touch all you say.
World that waits, you are too many things.
I have only a part, and I choose you,
persona, someone: come true, sing,
flame out, be me—who I might have been.[2]

What readers found in William Stafford's work was an attitude *toward* the world that provided a way of living *in* the world. Writing was a way of life. It was a way of being aware of others—and of nature; of moving toward his inevitable death. William Stafford's poems expand outward. They "burn into speech." But they burn quietly, slowly, like a fire that has been banked, ready for the future.

When William Stafford died on August 29, 1993, the literary world lost one of its most generous members. He had spent a lifetime teaching and talking about poetry, showing us how the quiet voice of a poem can change the world—if you listen well.

This book is a revised and expanded version of *Understanding William Stafford* (originally published by the University of South Carolina Press, 1989), which followed the course of Stafford's publications and noted not only his consistency, but also the development of new themes and concerns. Bill wrote his own "blurb" for that book, saying, "My poems tell me they like this book. True, they receive sympathy, but inside that embrace there is insight about their true heart and impulse. With this book they better their chances for finding congenial readers, always their aim, their ambition."[3] As the author, I was somewhat puzzled—his poems liked the book, but did he? However I also understood the characteristic modesty, the unwillingness to judge, the emphasis on the poetry rather than the poet himself. In this version, I have added to my original assessment of how the poems work, seeking to come even closer to their "true heart and impulse."

When a poet has died, especially an important poet—one who changed the shape of poetry and who helped to shape the work of others—there is a natural desire to read the work in its entirety, from beginning to end, in order to understand and assess its impact. When the poet is William Stafford, a man who wrote, perhaps, a poem a day for over forty years and published over sixty books during that time, we understand that no publisher could afford a complete Collected Poems and we'd happily settle for a good, comprehensive selection. Now Kim Stafford, his son and literary executor, has compiled just such a selection (*The Way It Is: New & Selected Poems*, Graywolf Press, 1998) so that readers and scholars alike can experience that written world.

This book is intended both as a comprehensive introduction for readers coming to Stafford seriously for the first time and as an overview of the work for those many readers already familiar with his poetry. It attempts to bring proportion and perspective to the extraordinarily large and varied work of a lifetime. It tries to open and explore what seem to me the most significant pathways into this rich oeuvre. Stafford invited us to "understand" his poems by understanding ourselves—our own relationship to language—with an honesty and insight that would match his own. "Suddenly this dream you are having matches / everyone's dream, and the result is the world."[4]

Judith Kitchen

1
Millions of Intricate Moves
Understanding William Stafford

Career

William Stafford spanned poetic generations. Born in 1914, chronologically belonging to the generation of Robert Lowell, Randall Jarrell, and John Berryman, older than Sylvia Plath, Stafford seemed to be the odd one out. Unlike the others, who could be termed "confessional" poets, Stafford appears to have chosen to write "personal" poetry; this includes a unique perspective coupled with a sense of moral and spiritual responsibility. He was what he himself termed a "witness for poetry."

William Edgar Stafford, first son of Earl Ingersoll and Ruby Mayher Stafford, was born in Hutchinson, Kansas. Raised in a nonconformist household, Stafford learned early the value of hard moral decisions and the security of firmly held convictions. Though neither parent formally belonged to a church, church was a central part of the social life of the small Kansas towns, and the family often attended services. His parents instilled in him a sense of justice, individuality, and tolerance. The oldest of three children, Stafford was close to each of his parents in different ways, looking to his father for gentle but firm guidance in ethical matters, to his mother for the more personal responses to everything from gossip to literature.

During the 1930s, while Stafford was an adolescent, his father moved the family from town to town within Kansas, following whatever jobs were available during the depth of the Depression. Within a small span of time, the Stafford family moved from Hutchinson to Wichita to Hutchinson to Liberal to Garden City to El Dorado. William carried his share of the load in each of these places, delivering papers (at one point the family's only source of income), raising vegetables, working in the sugar beet fields, and as an electrician's mate. During this time, he graduated from high school, went to Garden City and El Dorado Junior Colleges, and then enrolled at the University of Kansas where he worked his way through school waiting on tables. While at the university, Stafford began to take his writing seriously (mostly stories from the experiences he'd had moving from place to place). He also took seriously his social and political responsibilities, demonstrating against the policy of segregation in the Student Union cafe. In an essay written near the end of his life, he recalls a moment browsing in the university library when Nietzsche changed his world: "Sure, I was a reader. But this—this Nietzsche, these blazes of outrageous but tantalizing discovery . . ." In the same essay, Stafford speaks of other thinkers who made a difference to him (among them Pascal, Kierkegaard, George Eliot, Tolstoy, Gandhi, Goethe, Wittgenstein), and how the world "turned over," enlarged, and separated into "hundreds of little pieces."[1]

With the advent of World War II Stafford's convictions were tested. He registered as a pacifist (the commander of the American Legion of El Dorado spoke to the draft board in his behalf) and spent the duration of the war in camps and projects for conscientious objectors in Arkansas, California, and Illinois, working on soil conservation projects, forestry, and fighting fires. His choice was a courageous one. World War II was a popular war; to be a conscientious objector was to remove oneself from the mainstream of society. Stafford wrote, "My four years of 'alternative service under civilian direction' turned my life sharply into that independent channel of the second river—a course hereafter distinguished from any unexamined life, from the way it might have been in any of my hometowns."[2] It was during those years (1942-46) that Stafford developed the habit of spending the early part of the morning writing. Because his work was physically exhausting, it was impossible to write when he was through for the day. But he found he could always find an hour before work began. He carried this habit into marriage, fatherhood (he had four children), and a life of teaching.

The years spent in the Civilian Public Service were formative years; what had previously been belief hardened into practice. His emphasis on listening, his patience, his long-range goal of internal change—all stemmed from this period of his life. In addition, he developed a tool for survival—flexibility. Stafford learned to look hard at both sides of any question. In the end he emerged with a social vision that served him in his many other endeavors.

While still in the CO camps in southern California, Stafford met Dorothy Frantz, the daughter of a minister of the Church of the Brethren. They married, and Dorothy lived nearby, teaching in the public schools. When he was discharged from the Civilian Public Service in 1946 they could at last establish a home. Stafford finished a master's degree at the University of Kansas with the basic text of *Down in My Heart*, memoirs of the CO camps, forming his thesis; tried high school teaching in southern California; then moved to the San Francisco area to work for the Church World Service, a relief agency. During this time, *Down in My Heart* was published (1947) and Stafford continued to write each morning, publishing several poems in both small magazines and such distinguished literary journals as *Poetry*. In 1948 he was offered a teaching position at Lewis and Clark College in Portland, Oregon. He remained there until retirement, using Oregon as the base from which he could make occasional forays into the country at large.

One brief period away turned out to be of importance to his career as a writer. In 1950-52 Stafford worked on a writing degree at the University of Iowa, receiving his Ph.D. in 1954. Stafford was able to study under Paul Engle and to hear various writers such as Robert Penn Warren, Randall Jarrell, Reed Whittemore, and Karl Shapiro. Fellows writers in the program included W. D. Snodgrass and Donald Justice. He refers to these years as the "principal reference point I have for the literary life as lived by others."[3] Even then, he was putting some distance between his experience and that of his colleagues. For one thing, his experience of the war was wholly different from theirs; he was older, married, and had at that time two small children. His writing habits were established. But the courses and workshops at Iowa did have some effect; they served almost as a foil for the development of his own idiosyncratic attitudes toward the teaching of writing.

In 1960, eight years after he left Iowa, Robert Greenwood and Newton Baird asked to print some of Stafford's work with their newly formed Talisman Press, a small press in southern California—not, as he had hoped for, a major publishing company. *West of Your City*, Stafford's first book of poems, was published that year in a beautiful edition of a few hundred copies. At that time Stafford was forty-six years old.

Traveling Through the Dark, Stafford's second collection, was published by Harper and Row in 1962, and to some it must have seemed like a first book from a promising writer. It won the National Book Award for Poetry in 1963 and became fairly quickly a touchstone for a new generation of readers and poets who were looking for something different from the dominant mode of the "confessionals." Eight books from Harper and Row followed: *The Rescued Year* in 1966, *Allegiances* in 1970, *Someday, Maybe* in 1973, *Stories That Could Be True: New and Collected Poems* in 1977, *A Glass Face in the Rain* in 1982, *An Oregon Message* in 1987, and *Passwords* in 1991. Eight books in twenty-nine years would seem a prodigious amount from any poet, but this list represents only the titles from one publisher. Over forty other books or chapbooks of poetry, published by small presses; several books of prose, including essays on writing or writers, translations, talks; a poetic "dialogue" with Marvin Bell; and a reprint of *Down in My Heart* were also published in the quarter century following *Traveling Through the Dark*. In 1964 Stafford was awarded the Shelley Memorial Award from the Poetry Society of America, and in 1966 he received a Guggenheim fellowship. His prominence was confirmed in 1970 when he was named Consultant in Poetry for the Library of Congress. He traveled widely with the United States Information Service, reading in such countries as India, Pakistan, Iran, Egypt, and Thailand.

In the late 1960s and early 1970s, when unrest over the Vietnam War was at its height, students on campuses all over the country discovered the work of William Stafford. It seemed—in its pacifist leanings, its careful wisdom—to speak to and *for* them. Stafford was invited to read on campus after campus. This he did—Kent State, Berkeley, Madison, Hawaii to Alaska—but it was not always what either he or the students had expected. He was truly a non-violent man, and the antiwar demonstrators were at times disposed to a violent method of making their views known. Stafford was uncomfortable with the role of spokesman, but he was still willing to be a witness. He said, of this time, "Both sides spread out leaving pacifists where they usually were, alone."[4] His easy-going, conversational reading style became one more statement about the place of poetry in a difficult and despairing world.

In 1980 Stafford retired from teaching, but not from the world of poetry. He published three new major collections and was given the Award in Literature by the American Academy and Institute of Arts and Letters. In 1991 he was awarded a National Endowment for the Arts Senior Fellowship for a lifetime of "extraordinary contributions to American literature." In addition, his collection, *My Name Is William Tell*, published by Confluence Press, was the winner of the 1992 Western States Book Award Lifetime Achievement in Poetry. What might have mattered to him most, however, was the selection by the National Park Service of seven poems from his "Methow River" series which have been etched and mounted on road signs along the North Cascades Highway in Washington state. His sudden and unexpected death in 1993 left hundreds of poems in manuscript, a selection (chosen by Robert Bly) in page proofs, and a posthumous collection entitled *Even in Quiet Places* which collects poems from recent chapbooks along with the previously unpublished poems from the Methow River series. Many of the poems from his last year, including some overt antiwar poems engendered by the Gulf War, are finally available in *The Way It Is*.

Even though Stafford has not yet had the critical attention he deserves, "Traveling Through the Dark" has become the most widely anthologized contemporary poem. His influence, not only on the teaching of writing, but on what to expect from poetry itself, has quietly grown. It is only now that other poets are beginning to realize just how great an effect William Stafford and his poetry have had on their way of looking at the world.

Overview

William Stafford's complete work constitutes a testament for living. At first reading, it might appear to recall an almost idyllic childhood, to reflect a lifetime of longing for the past—a harking back to a time that was simpler, when people could make peace with nature, when Indians lived in harmony with the world. But his poems are aimed, deliberately, at modern humans with the bomb hanging over their heads. How to live in a world like ours? Stafford consistently notes the ways in which our technology threatens to sever us from our humanity. His answer is not the stereotypical "nature as salvation"; his poems exhibit complex and complicated relationships—between people, between humans and the land, between the public and the private person. In "Representing Far Places" he concludes, "It is all right to be simply the way you have to be,/ among contradictory ridges in some crescendo of knowing."[5] This "permission" that he gives himself feels hard-won, as though wrested from deep doubt.

What underlies all Stafford's poetry is a fixed vision. Stafford himself would have balked at the use of a word like *fixed*, careful as he was to test all sides of a question, to entertain all possible meanings. But *fixed* may be broad enough (certain without being rigid) to encompass the idea of flexibility and to make room for change. In that context, it was firmly held convictions, as well as a clarity of vision, that gave Stafford the strength to roam freely in his imagination and to test every aspect of his vision.

This vision seems to have crystallized during the four years spent in CO camps during World War II. William Stafford spent formative years of his youth tucked away in the backwoods of the country, digging ditches, building bridges, learning to find his way in uneasy situations, learning to speak softly but firmly for what he believed to be the truth. He emerged with a mature sensibility that characterized both his writing and his teaching; he was patient, receptive, ready to learn. In the 1985 foreword to *Down in My Heart*, which he entitled "A Side Glance at History," Stafford looked back at that time: "Back then—and now—one group stays apart from the usual ways of facing war. They exist now—and they did then— in all countries. Those who refuse the steps along that way are a small group, and their small role is a footnote in the big histories."[6] But Stafford considered, in hindsight, that theirs was a significant role. He continued to play the role in the writing of his poetry— not that he wrote polemical or cautionary poetry, but that he allowed himself to "stay apart" and make small noises for the good of humankind, the good *in* humankind. Stafford himself chronicled the connection between that period of his life and his writing: "We were surrounded by challenges that had to do with that tension between open, ordinary daily life and the interior life that distinguishes individuals from each other. The two parts of my life that blended or clashed in making my writing were in constant alertness. I felt my morning writings as maintenance work or repair work on my integrity."[7]

If Stafford's vision is considered as having coalesced around his conscientious objector's experience, then it is possible to look at the subsequent poetry to see just what the angle of that vision is. This is subtle work, since Stafford's glance was always sideways and his work slanted toward meaning rather than embodied it directly. The natural world serves as a source of imagery, but often it is an imagery that is general, even abstract—stone, bird, tree, as opposed to granite, chickadee, elm. The imagery, especially as it recurs, becomes symbolic. The "ideas" do reside in the "things,"[8] but the things are often blurred by their generality or by qualifying adjectives and skewed uses of verbs. To enter Stafford's world, it is necessary to step lightly, to follow his footsteps over unmarked snow, to be receptive to the small sounds and the fleeting moments that hold a mystery, and a delight.

It is possible to view William Stafford's work, more than the work of most other poets, as if it had been written all at once. It appears to come from a central, unchanging sensibility. That this sensibility can seem to change so little is most likely due to the fact that it is a sensibility that accepts change, or flux, as part of its natural method. The quest is how to encompass separate aspects (the two rivers) of the self into a unified, and unique, vision. It is difficult to tell poems that were first printed in *West of Your City* from poems that appeared over twenty-five years later in *An Oregon Message*. Both the themes and the methods remained consistent. Scattered throughout all of his books is a mixture of biographical poems rooted in his personal life, and other, less factual poems where his imagination has led him to a persona or to the stance of the more distanced observer. Because the poems have this "mix and match" property, they have been variously collected by editors according to theme or chronology or central concern. In each case the collection works as a whole. This study will follow Stafford's major publications as they appeared chronologically, attempting to piece together an unfolding understanding (on the part of the reader) of his larger vision.

Stafford was not as young as many of his "generation" when he first published his poetry. His first trade edition came out in 1962, but it must be noted that it won him immediate critical attention and acclaim. At this time Lowell's watershed book, *Life Studies*, had been in print for three years. Stafford and Lowell shared the experience of refusing to fight in World War II, but they differed dramatically on how they would use that experience in their poetry. Lowell's militantly defiant stance seemed anathema to Stafford's temperament, with its nearly invisible thrust toward a pacifistic way of thinking. In fact, both thematically and stylistically, Stafford seemed to share more with a slightly younger generation; he belongs to the poetic generation that includes James Wright, Robert Bly, Richard Hugo, and Donald Hall, among others. Both his themes and his style place him as a transitional poet, between generations.

Stafford could be characterized as a poet of the ordinary. For him, small things often have their own historical significance. What is eventful may be something that is hardly noticed; the poet's task is to notice, and to listen. Out of this listening, several dominant themes emerge in the work; these themes could be characterized as threads which, woven together, make up the intricate tapestry of a lifetime's work. There is his concern with family and home which extends to the past (and therefore time in general). Another thread is that of the West, which is, for him, equated with the wilderness and a communion with nature (and, by extension, his eventual death). Still another concern is technology and the accompanying fear that the nation will fail to put it to its proper uses. These themes, however, are all part of a larger vision. Stafford is not afraid to commit himself to moral values; the poems examine the origin of these values and, at the same time, apply them to the present and the future. In writing, he is learning how to live—and how to die.

It is impossible to look at Stafford's poems and how they work without taking into account some of his statements about the writing process itself. Luckily, he was always free with these opinions and his essays have been collected in three volumes for the University of Michigan's Poets On Poetry series. In *You Must Revise Your Life* (1986), Stafford's introductory essay, entitled

"Sources and Resources," states, "For me an artist is someone who lets the material talk back." He goes on to say, "I wanted to disappear as teacher, as writer, as citizen—be 'the quiet of the land,' as we used to designate ourselves in CO camps."[9]

The habit of disappearing, of letting the material speak, led Stafford to an "immediate engagement with the language."[10] Rather than beginning with an idea, Stafford advocates beginning anywhere, with anything, and letting the idea develop through a series of moves, what he terms almost a dance. To do this, the poet must be receptive—even passive—so that the ideas or possibilities inherent in the images can assert themselves. "My progressions are perhaps provable after the fact, but I don't progress because I think they're going to be provable. I progress by hunches and echoes."[11] If one writes this way, the writing is the discovery, and the surprise at where the poem has gone is shared by writer and reader alike.

In *Writing the Australian Crawl* (1978), Stafford compares the making of a poem to starting a car on ice. Rather than revving the motor, the driver must ease the car into motion; the same is true for poems:

> If you compose a poem you start without any authority. . . . But a poet—whatever you are saying, and however you are saying it, the only authority you have builds from the immediate performance, or it does not build.

> If the reader or listener enters the poem, I want the moves to come from inside the poem, the coercion to be part of the life right there.

> Someplace he [Auden] said he feared repeating himself as the years went by, and this fear shocked me, for it undercut a view I have long cherished—that a writer is not trying for a product, but accepting sequential signals and adjustments toward an always-arriving present. To slight that readiness—even in order to avoid repetition—would be to violate the process, would be to make writing into a craft that neglected its contact with the ground of its distinction.[12]

The essays are filled with a pithy wisdom. Lines can be lifted almost at random to demonstrate how solidly Stafford stands behind the principle of receptivity:

> Poetry is the kind of thing you have to see from the corner of your eye.
>
> A poem is a serious joke, a truth that has learned *jujitsu*.
>
> Literature is not a picture of life, but is a separate experience with its own kind of flow and enhancement.
>
> A person writes by means of that meager but persistent little self he has with him all the time.[13]

Stafford's willingness to accept signals and to listen to his "little self" has resulted in poems that feel their way into their material. What happens inside the poem is often quiet, almost imperceptible. But something happens. The transformations in Stafford's poetry seem to take place off the page but enter the meaning of the poem. For this reason, George Lensing and Ronald Moran have included him in their study of poets of "the emotive imagination."[14] They rightly assess this accumulation of associative images, and the leap of imagination that fuses them, as being like similar strategies in Robert Bly and James Wright. For Stafford, though, the truth does not lie in the images themselves, but in the linkage of specific images with an *idea* of the world. And it is always a moment in this world that reveals the other world. As Peter Stitt observes in a review of *A Glass Face in the Rain*, "Stafford's gaze is not turned upon any world other than this one."[15]

In an essay entitled "Some Arguments Against Good Diction," Stafford makes clear that he believes that language shapes the event, not the other way around. In fact, he recounts his "distrust" of words, especially as conveyors of "truth." He goes on to say:

> . . . the transaction also begins to enhance the experience because of a weird quality in language: the successive distortions of language have their own kind of cumulative potential, and under certain conditions the distortions of language can reverberate into new experiences more various,

more powerful, and more revealing than the experiences that set off language in the first place.[16]

This receptivity to distortion results in interesting verbal constructions ("Under my hat I custom you intricate, Ella"[17]; leaves "numbering along through summer"[18]), occasional striking adjectives ("free-spending sycamores"[19]; "hysterical water"[20]), and somewhat nebulous statements that suggest a meaning beyond explication ("And a world begins under the map"[21]). Synesthesia, or mixing of the senses, is one element of this distortion, as though precise description would somehow miss the "feel" of the moment: "a touch/ of light survived in amethyst."[22] Personification, too, allows the poems to try out new modes of perception: "four bicycles/ in line unreeling their shadows."[23]; "sunlight stretches out its limbs."[24] He deliberately slants meaning in order to "get it right." Such openness to these possibilities in language admits contradictory ideas as well. In fact, Stafford is best read by looking for the countless opposites that his poems contain. His basic concerns are doubled and redoubled as he explores the dual nature of language and life.

Light and dark, lake and sky, present and past, sound and sight, near and far, rational and intuitive—all are included, often simultaneously, in the world of his poetry. The polarities of mother and father are explored; he sees two sides of himself—the judgmental, fearful side and the receptive, open side. One poem, "Vocation," seems to sum up this underlying tension:

> This dream the world is having about itself
> includes a trace on the plains of the Oregon trail,
> a groove in the grass my father showed us all
> one day while meadowlarks were trying to tell
> something better about to happen.
>
> I dreamed the trace to the mountains, over the hills,
> and there a girl who belonged wherever she was.
> But then my mother called us back to the car:
> she was afraid; she always blamed the place,
> the time, anything my father planned.

> Now both of my parents, the long line through the
>   plain,
> the meadowlarks, the sky, the world's whole dream
> remain, and I hear him say while I stand between the
>   two,
> helpless, both of them part of me:
> "Your job is to find what the world is trying to be."[25]

Not only does the poem include the contrasting attitudes of the parents, it also characterizes Stafford's representation of time. The trace is ancient, from a history that can't be uncovered except as it leaves its "trace," and it persists in the present. The memory is of a past action when the father "showed" and the mother "called." But the poem itself takes place in the present—the third stanza begins with the word *now*. The world's dream "about itself," as it moves through time, is the larger dream that includes the individual dreams of its inhabitants (in this instance, the speaker's dream of a girl); the writer stands between the dream and the world as it manifests itself, trying to find out what to make of what happens, or is about to happen. The speaker begins in the present, looking back, and then ends in a present tense that is buried within that past. The poem mediates between two times—the intensely felt moment of the poem and the past that persists into the present. He is called in both directions, out into the world and back to the safety of family. The vocation of writing is truly a calling—internal, through personal necessity; external, through listening hard to whatever message is out there.

"Both of them part of me." The mother and father figures permeate Stafford's poetry. There is a side that wants to name, to blame, to speak out, both for and *against*. There is another side that honors his father's essence, wanting to feel its way toward meaning, willing to listen and discover and believe. This internal war is reflected in his language. Every word contains the shadow of its opposite, and this is particularly true in the work of William Stafford.

The willingness to be part of the world and, at the same time, the recognition that the world is a cold, indifferent place to be, forces Stafford to find a world of his own. This world is understood by recognizing its specific vocabulary. Some words become symbolic or, at the very least, invested with an overtone of extended meaning. The reader develops a shorthand through which to read the poems, especially as these words recur in changing patterns and combinations. Common objects begin to function in specific ways: home is associated with self, river with change, snow with the page, wires with communication. Certain verbs take on idiosyncratic meanings: seeing is equated with knowing, listening with understanding. The poems move to the edge of meaning, a quiet brinksmanship. *Edge* becomes one of those charged words. The world creates those edges; people test themselves in the face of the abyss. *Swerve*, too, becomes a word with heightened meaning. It almost always is used in a double sense, a movement in the physical world and a mental motion where the true action of the poem takes place.

This doubleness extends to the land, and for Stafford this is very significant. In a manner reminiscent of Whitman, he celebrates the land and its people. Speaking for the earth, he says, "have a place, be what that place / requires."[26] He sees two kinds of lives—the surface, everyday life, on earth, and the life that is evidenced "under" the earth, "deep, the way it is."[27] Subterranean caves, underground streams, animals in their burrows—these are the physical embodiments in the poems that represent this deeper place in the earth (and in the self), where meaningful events take place in isolation and silence. The poet must feel his way back to an original source: "Inside: the universe that happens."[28] The quest for even a glimpse of this interior "state" is at the heart of most of Stafford's poetry.

In what he later refers to as a "dream vision," the young Stafford had an experience that changed his life. While still in high school, he biked twelve miles to camp on the banks of the Cimarron River. He spent the day, and the following night, watching as the sun fell and rose again. "No person anywhere, nothing, just space, the solid earth. . . . That encounter with the size and serenity of the earth and its neighbors in the sky has never left me. The earth was my home; I would never feel lost while it held me."[29] In Stafford's poetry there is often an attempt to duplicate, at least in feeling, that original dream vision. Often, when this happens, the "earth" becomes the "world," and a distinction is made between the *place* of living and a larger, natural order which governs all life. "Starting

With Little Things" begins by admonishing "Love the earth like a mole" and ends with the promise "Tomorrow the world."[30] This subtle but important transformation mirrors the knowledge gained in that one evening on the Cimarron.

Beyond sight, in the realm of the invisible, imagination is possible. In Stafford's poetry this usually takes place under cover of darkness. Imagination is so essential that it leads to a nearly religious experience. Something exists beyond human comprehension; imagination puts a person in touch with that larger possibility. Perhaps the most difficult concept to understand in the work of William Stafford is this religious moment. Although Stafford had no formal religion, the poems contain many words associated with the Quaker faith. For example, *witness* is used in all its senses. He is witness *to* injustice, to history as it is being made; and he is witness *for* alternatives, for values, a way of thinking as well as a way of living. The idea of balance is paramount. *Friend*, too, is a common word, extending beyond the personal to a human fellowship. The silent communion of the meeting house is echoed in Stafford's silent communion with nature. He faces himself, looking inward. All this suggests the religious nature of the work, and a method by which the reader can mine the larger implications in a poem that is, on the surface, somewhat transparent.

The use of the word *God* often parallels his use of the word *dream*. The untitled poem included in the essay "Whose Tradition?" is a good example. "There is a dream going on while I am awake,"[31] he says. This is the "perpetual dream" in which each individual participates; for want of a better word, Stafford sometimes (but not always) refers to this idea as "God" or "prayer" or "truth." He often surrounds the word *dream* with a vocabulary associated with religion. Whatever else, this suggests some sense of an eternal, sustaining force which implies as well an ultimate purpose: the dream persists even after death: "When I die, the dream is the only / thing left." When an individual life coincides with that larger, ongoing dream there is a moment of grace, a "blending / of our chance selves with what sustains / all chance." To embody the dream is to become part of the sublime. In this sense, Stafford's work could be called religious, but the religion is highly individual and its tenets can be found only in the body of the work. There is, beyond this sense of the religious, a sense of the mystical, seen most often when the poems hover on the verge of knowing. The poems hesitate, surge forward, circle around something that remains undefined. The world reveals itself, the poem turns, then quietly goes on.

Time, for Stafford, is more a concern than a theme. It is both fluid and fixed. Acutely aware of flux, Stafford finds several ways to recapture the present. The lyric moment becomes his focus— the lived present with its felt emotions and its feeling toward meaning, as opposed to the clarity of hindsight. In the early poems this concern with time shows up in the tense of the poem and a characteristic "slippage" between tenses. Time is seen to be cyclical, and layered:

> We stand
> inside a curve, inside long lines
> that make a more secret curve.[32]

It is something we live within. But the later poems address Time as though it were a character in its own right, with its own properties: "Time is back in its cage."[33] In 1988 Stafford published eight poems in *The Ohio Review* under the title "Finding Our Way." In one way or another these poems demonstrate this altered sense of time. Time locks us all within the confines of an individual life, and yet it also hints at a "different country"—possibly an alternative life, certainly something we live *without*. Mesh, calendar squares, prison bars, screen, lace—the matrices of time catch and hold us, while its motion is a "sideways drift." And if only the "now" is real, at least it is a now that contains a "then":

> It's a country where
> you already are, bringing where you have been.[34]

Stafford's poems are often about the process of their own creation. To this end they allow themselves to meander. The language is often simple—even deceptively so. Stafford has been described as a sort of mid-western Robert Frost; the similarities are there, but not in the way the description suggests. Each poet worked hard to create an easy, colloquial speech pattern and to be receptive to the cadences of the spoken word. Stafford often started a poetry reading by talking and then suddenly moving into the poem. It took the audience approximately one stanza to recognize that the subtle shift had been made. Like Frost, Stafford looks hard at the world, and often the world comes up wanting. The dark side is explored under the guise of what might seem like innocuous images. Each poet has been misunderstood, thought of as a "nature" poet with simple observations about the world, when actually each of them, from a unique vantage point, has handed his public a bleak, sometimes cruel, picture of the world's indifference. Frost often used words like "fear" or "scare," but Stafford speaks of "terror." This points to an inner darkness, a sense of man's capacity to hurt others, where he sometimes finds himself terrified by what he knows of *human* nature.

Often Stafford's poetry pushes us "over the edge," into that dark—and lonely—moral limbo where the isolated individual is called on to wrestle with an individual conscience. The "dream" you are having that "matches / everyone's dream" is *not* a shared ideology, but a dream of shared individuality. In moments of grace where people find a way to live within their own uncertain times, Stafford's poems, like Frost's, rise to a simple eloquence and offer a message of hope.

The message, for Stafford, is more in the forward motion of the poem than in what the poem ultimately "says." The poet is often likened to a walker, someone leaving prints/tracks/trails/marks on the world. He discovers his own road and makes his own map. Process is so important to Stafford that many of his poems embody his theories of writing—the way poems find out what they are about. The pace is often slow, including what looks like non-sequiturs (what he termed "being distracted in a positive direction"[35]). This sometimes makes the poem feel "talky," and the reader would like to hurry it to its point. But its point is in its method of discovering itself, and that often involves letting the various elements come together to suggest a deeper connection. This might imply a lack of craft, but the opposite is almost always the case; the craft has been subsumed in favor of the process.

For Stafford, craft, in the sense of traditional poetic forms, was simply too easy. It offered him no challenge. It is clear that he had a natural ear, wrote easily in form and with a near-perfect rhythmical cadence. His poems consistently fought against this natural ability, working toward a much more complex sense of rhythm and rhyme than the conventional sonnet would call for. This was partly due to his belief that tradition should also include the spoken word—its inflections and variations and subtle changes—as well as the "literary" tradition. "Poetry is not a going back, but a going forward."[36] Stafford's sense of craft was one that moved from, and enlarged, literary tradition. He was a master of subliminal rhymes, variations on expected meters, and a syncopation of line which calls attention to specific words—and silences.

Stafford's work has been characterized by critic Jonathan Holden as belonging to a convention he terms the "contemporary conversation poem."[37] There is an easy, even intimate, conversational style, stories to be told, thoughts to be examined. Some poems seem to speak directly to the reader, or audience, often employing the device of direct address. Almost all of them use a colloquial speech pattern. A closer look, though, shows an unanticipated distance between writer and reader. Certainly the language invites, but the poems hold the reader off with an abstraction of both image and idea and a curious lack of detail. This resistance is sustained by the use of certain rhetorical and poetic devices, not the least of which is sound. Stafford weaves a dense tapestry, or pattern, of sound throughout his poems, alerting the ear to the formal aspects of his work. In this way, he can pretend to let readers directly into his most private thoughts, but the poem itself serves as a sort of mask, fending them off even as it calls out a welcome. To participate one must do more than listen as the story unfolds; one must discover how to enter the imaginative landscape that the sounds, as well as the images, are defining.

In the end, the poems are about love—about daring to love under hard circumstances and in difficult times. They are an acceptance of duty—a duty to "find a place,"[38] a duty to be of, and for, the earth. Readers who follow Stafford through more than a thousand poems, accepting the "signals" as Stafford accepted them, will find insight into the human condition. They will experience the world in all its facets, will face the dark and the light. "A writer is not so much someone who has something to say as he is someone who has found a process that will bring about new things he would not have thought of if he had not started to say them."[39] The "new things" are the poems; in the case of William Stafford, the poems make whole new worlds to explore.

Stafford and the Critics

Over the years that William Stafford was writing, critical fashion changed. When he attended the Writing Program at the University of Iowa, New Criticism was at its height. By the late 1980s, he had watched the rise (and at least partial fall) of structuralism and various post-modernisms, including deconstruction. Throughout this evolution Stafford's own work remained consistent, but the manner in which it has been read by these movements has varied. Under some of these methods of criticism his work cannot receive much critical attention since it does not readily fit the requirements of the movement.

The simple language and the unstrained quality of Stafford's poems led to misunderstanding. Like Frost before him, Stafford was most interested in a wide audience of sympathetic readers; to gain that audience he studiedly avoided the appearance of being too esoteric or "difficult." With some critics he may have become the victim of his own quest for a readership of "ordinary" people. The seeming simplicity of his subject matter and his conversational tone gained the wrong kind of attention from some scholars.

"You see / intricate but fail at simple" says Stafford, in "Seeing and Perceiving."[40] He is accusing himself, noting a human failing, but the statement could easily be leveled at literary critics. It is difficult to write about the simple, and most of his critics have failed at this task. Reviews of his work rely on characteristic phrases such as "unassuming tone" and "natural modesty." It has been easy for reviewers to note the colloquial speech patterns without fully analyzing their effect and, even more, why Stafford was using them. Unfortunately many critics have also equated "simple" with "unimportant." Also, Stafford's refusal to "edit" his own work and to limit the amount he published caused critics to take him less seriously than they should have. Stephen Corey, writing in *The Virginia Quarterly Review*, warned him of this, saying "Recurrent ideas can become repetitive poems."[41]

Critics have tended to view Stafford in one of two categories: as a poet of place or as a poet of myth. Sanford Pinsker acknowledges Stafford's roots in Kansas, but looks to the imagery and attitudes (even psychology) that makes him a "northwestern" poet. Pinsker does not want to call Stafford a regional poet (knowing that Stafford would have resisted the label), so he cites the Indian myth poems as examples of his identification with the region. In the end Pinsker is forced to read Stafford's poems in a broader context, discovering their universal properties; "Wonder brings him to his poems, and it is there that he has said God's plenty about the light and darkness of our condition, and about the constant amazement and tentative truths we all share."[42]

George Lensing and Ronald Moran emphasize the "mythic" in *Four Poets of the Emotive Imagination*. This particular reading of Stafford looks at the father figure as archetypal, the westward "journey" as Jungian. The emphasis is on the transcendent moment when, in an intuitive leap, the poet discerns in the wilderness what is otherwise concealed. But Lensing and Moran note that Stafford does not quite fit their prescriptive formula. If Stafford can be called mythic, it is in the sense that he created his *own* mythology, composed of the elements of being (time, space, earth, air, water), and his sense of how personal history fits within human history.

The Mark to Turn by Jonathan Holden, published in 1976, is an excellent study of Stafford's first five books. Holden was certainly the first, and perhaps only, critic to note what he calls Stafford's "interlocking set of metaphors." In defining for himself the specific vocabulary of the poems, Holden builds a strong case for the coherence of the body of the work and recognizes a similarity with Wallace Stevens: "Like Stevens's, Stafford's Romanticism is stylized, abstract, and always informed by a controlling intelligence."[43]

Very late in Stafford's career, Tom Andrews edited a collection— *On William Stafford: The Worth of Local Things*—for the University of Michigan's Under Discussion series. It contains a number of reviews, general essays, and essays on particular poems or articles by such critics and writers as James Dickey, Laurence Lieberman, Richard Howard, Peter Stitt, Fred Chappell, Donald Hall, Henry Taylor, Linda Pastan, and David Young, providing an excellent overview of critical appraisals over the years and demonstrating a range of opinions. It could be said that each reader encounters a different William Stafford—and each feels strongly that his or her Stafford should be understood by others.

One contemporary critic, Charles Altieri, uses Stafford as a foil for a larger argument. In *Self and Sensibility in Contemporary American Poetry*, Altieri claims that American poetry of the 70s had been dominated, and enervated, by what he terms "the scenic style."[44] He defines this as poetry characterized by the sensibility of the poet, supposedly present in a specific "real" scene (geographic or emotional or both) in which the poet's insights are allowed to become a sufficient justification for the poem. In such poetry, Altieri argues, craft and sensibility are taken as ultimate values, the reader is manipulated, and the means of poetry remain as unquestioned as its ends. There is no room for a "dialectical thinking" about what Altieri sees as the truly important issues; language is taken for granted in the service of a "smug, self-satisfied lyrical persona constantly transported into visionary states by the poet's apt metaphors or turns of events."[45]

But how well does this fit Stafford? Altieri, choosing one very early Stafford poem ("Ceremony" from *West of Your City*), notes in this poem an "imposed congruence" and the "controlling hand of the craftsman." These, he feels, are subtly used to try to express the "inexpressible." The result is, according to Altieri, an artifical "naturalness" used only to convey this "scenic effect." What Altieri would like, however, is a poet who feels the "responsibility to reflect upon the rhetorical figures producing the poem's moment of vision."[46] In other words, Stafford is not philosopher enough for Altieri's taste.

This is an example of the damage done by taking a Stafford poem out of its larger context. If Altieri were not intent on making his own arguments, he might have read further only to discover that Stafford was more aware than most of his contemporaries that meaning does lie outside as well as inside language. His poems demonstrate that awareness over and over. The body of Stafford's work is an example of dialectical thinking; the "controlling hand" that Altieri so dislikes is only one piece of the evidence that Stafford is well aware of the double bind in writing.

In fact, Stafford's intuitive sense of the rift between reality and language may lie at the heart of his refusal to be his own critic. He recognized the "faker"—the writer of the poem—within himself. His desperate need to protect his writing self from his critical self may well have led him to his controversial theories of non-intervention. This is revealed in a *Northwest Review* discussion with Richard Hugo, who suspected early that Stafford was a "shrewd judge" of his own work.[47] Hugo responds to a statement by Stafford that maybe "the world happens three times":

> *Hugo:* But when you say things like that, you start leaving the poem. Those are footnotes. . . .
>
> *Stafford:* Well, maybe the poem says that, but in my life I really want to say the world happens three times: once what I superficially see, second what I do my best to see, and third what I suspect I'll never be able to see it as.
>
> *Hugo:* Right. Maybe the better way to put it is that the world happens three times; two of them you can use in poems.
>
> *Stafford:* Yeah, the third time is when you take the poem apart and say, Here's the faker inside the poem.
>
> *Hugo:* And that third way is the way of the critic.[48]

Stafford goes on in the interview to say that it's "dangerous" to look at poems when they have been completed because "you can out-think yourself." Perhaps Stafford's greatest fear was this ability to out-think himself; to give in to the critic might be to lose the poems before they came to fruition.

Typically, Stafford revealed this fear in a roundabout way throughout his poetry. The "logical ones" that he resisted in favor of another way of "knowing" may have been the flip side of himself. His wry wit and the way he often turned his poems back on their speaker would indicate that he sensed this: "But awaking from awaking, I am a little man myself crying, / 'Faker! Faker!'"[49]; "Last I accuse— / Myself: my terrible poise."[50] He looks hard, and with suspicion, at his own judgmental nature. The source of the tension that creates the poems may be his desire *not* to judge in the face of his natural inclinations. *Judgment* is, therefore, one more highlighted word in Stafford's linking vocabulary. He notes his own tendency to be a bit didactic about others, and at the same time he manages to be highly self-critical. Often he projects this tendency onto the landscape itself so that the judgment seems to be coming from the large impersonal force of nature. In all this he has been careful to turn his own judgment inward, and there he has found justice as well as accusation—the "silence and the judgment of the sky."[51]

That Stafford knew which of his poems were perhaps the finest is made clear, in an indirect fashion, in a short essay published in *The Ohio Review* not long before his death. Talking about how important the act of reading was in his life, and honoring the excitement he felt when he first read Nietzsche, he moved to a discussion of his own process. In doing so, he quoted three of his most important lines, from three of his best poems:

> And in my writing, I feel the presence of that new continent, an influence more pervasive and important than any consideration of writing craft: "Traveling through the dark I found a deer . . .," "In the late night listening from bed I have joined the ambulance or the patrol . . .," "Ask me mistakes I have made. . . ." These glimpses, to me, have the flavor of that new world.[52]

William Stafford's poems are about survival in a complex, even threatening, world. The poems themselves survive in a complicated critical milieu. They will outlast both poetic and critical fashion because, in them, Stafford has looked for, and found, the "self which endures." That self may be best described by his own dream of the perfect reading, ending in a unifying vision that is almost, but not quite, an assertion:

> What would be dear to me would be not to enter and make an impression or leave and be forgotten—either of those— but to have it be like something that happens and you don't know what it is and after it's over you still don't know; nevertheless, something has happened.

I would like the poems to be like that too. Instead of having all the effects of the poem be recognized while I'm there, I would like them just to linger after I've gone, and no one needs to know what happened.[53]

2

The Whole Land's Wave
Down in My Heart and *West of Your City*

Down in My Heart

In 1947 William Stafford published his first book, entitled *Down in My Heart*, a collection of prose memoirs of the time he spent in CO camps during World War II. Only recently has it been possible to test his poetry against the stated convictions contained in this account. Until 1985 it had been circulated by The Brethren Publishing House and had found its way more to political and social thinkers than to lovers of literature. With its reprinting by The Bench Press (1985) and the excerpts in *The Georgia Review* (Winter 1984), this valuable biographical collection became far better known. Oregon State University Press has now issued a further reprint (1998), thus keeping this literary legacy alive.

Down in My Heart is a spiritual biography. Stafford gave up four years for his conviction that killing people can never solve problems between people. He spent those years in hard work, but also in hard thought. This book chronicles his confusions, his doubts, and his discoveries, along with his growing sense of isolation. *Down in My Heart* is a book about ideas and relationships and how the two intertwine. The men entered the camps in 1942 with a sense that they could make a statement to their country; they left in 1946 with a feeling of failure—and a sense that their war had only just begun. Their war was a war against hatred, injustice, ignorance, poverty, violence, and their mission was to promote change in the way society viewed these problems.

"When are men dangerous?" asks Stafford in an early episode, "The Mob Scene at McNeil."[1] Three men had walked to an Arkansas town on a Sunday—to paint, to write, to read. But the very presence of the men was an affront to the patriotic citizenry, and soon an angry mob formed. Countrymen angry at countrymen, words like *lynching* could be heard. That time they were saved—as Stafford tells us—by Walt Whitman. Some of the mob believed that the men were spies, not poets, since what they were writing did not rhyme. Stafford was carrying a copy of *Leaves of Grass*, and he managed to convince the group that free verse was also poetry. An understanding sheriff saw them safely home. Other times they saved themselves using the techniques of nonviolence. But the psychic assault was always there; they felt hated by the very country they loved. They learned to keep in mind a larger country—a human brotherhood. When, on 6 August 1945, Stafford heard about the atomic bomb, he did not describe it as falling on a Japanese city, but "that we had dropped a new kind of deadly bomb on a city of Japanese people."[2]

These memoirs demonstrate, with subtlety, the growing isolation of the men in the camps. With this isolation came a fierce independence and a sure sense of the self in the world. Stafford's questioning voice and subsequent insight is best seen in a short passage from "Mountain Conscription":

> What spirit had we by now in our hearts? And what was the
> power thereof? We were together to start another chapter
> under conscription. . . . Outside was a universally serrate
> scene: far off, the jagged peaks; nearer, the intervening,
> overlapping, wooded peaks; and right at hand, extending for
> miles in every direction, the incredibly detailed work of pine
> after pine, slope after slope. Those surroundings had
> enclosed, at the same camp just before this season, prisoners
> from Folsom State—paid prisoners as we called them, who
> had done the same kind of work planned for us, and who
> had stolen some cars and engaged in enough Susanville vice
> to give our camp a reputation to begin on. We were starting
> a home again, but in a way, by this time, we were carrying a
> home with us.[3]

The idea of "home" as residing in the interior self, independent of place but fully integrated with a sense of the ideal, begins here. The larger vision that Stafford exhibits in the body of his poetry is centered around this definition of home and what it means to be an individual.

The sense of isolation persisted throughout a lifetime; in a 1989 videotape entitled "What the River Says," Stafford recalled the years spent as a conscientious objector—a time he referred to as being "out in the cold, for four crucial years":

> The automatic assumption that one didn't have to conform—
> in fact conformity was a danger sign—I fought against that.
> I wanted to be a part of society, but I think the steady
> realization that one could be different and apart in a day-by-
> day basis without questioning oneself about it couldn't help
> having an influence on the writing habits and on the habits
> of mind that made you different from—and ready to be
> different from—the society around you.[4]

West of Your City

Although *Down in My Heart* was published right after the war, Stafford's first book of poems did not appear until thirteen years later. The poems in *West of Your City* (1960) draw on some of the attitudes expressed in the earlier prose work and, at the same time, establish what turned out to be life-long themes and concerns. At the age of forty-six, Stafford began his poetic career with a mature voice—a voice that began by looking back. "Mine was a Midwest home—you can keep your world," begins "One Home,"[5] and Stafford evokes the Kansas plains, a history that encompasses his grandfather, wildcats, Indians, the "plain black hats" of the stoic, religious people who settled there. The final line—"Wherever we looked the land would hold us up."—echoes his epiphany on the banks of the Cimarron and shows why "you can keep your world." His Midwestern childhood held a sense of security in the moral codes and the settled land, and a sense of adventure at the edges— the wilderness yet to be explored. The earth itself becomes his home.

Home becomes the theme for this book, and the loss of home becomes its obsession. The poems often use the first person, both singular and plural. The persona (or speaker) of the poem and the poet (especially where biographical fact is used) are nearly identical, but the poet/speaker extends his personal experience to include others. There is a deliberate attempt to find correspondence between the individual life of the writer and the shared life of the community. Community extends to the natural world, especially animals. In "Ceremony" Stafford describes how a muskrat bit his hand under the bank of the Ninnescah River. The blood is described as "something the ocean would remember" (30, *61*). In this moment of recognition, the moment of scarring, the persona of the poem realizes that all of life is fluid, that some part of him will reach the ocean from the middle of this vast country. The moment has held meaning not only for him, but for the muskrat as well; all of nature is affected by this encounter with the human. The muskrat bites him on "the third finger of my left hand"—a "marriage" of the human and the natural world. This poem roots him in his native Kansas plains but foreshadows his embracing all of the land. Here, the river—fluid, deep, endless—is established as one of Stafford's natural images. In poem after poem, rivers, their currents and hidden depths, become natural symbols for movement, and mystery. They are the places he will look for meaning.

Once the home has been established, the whole of *West of Your City* seems to be a returning, for one reason or another. "Circle of Breath" recreates the night of his father's death, and Stafford describes himself as driving east, "truant from knowing" (32, *62*). Ignorance of the fact of the death allows him to remember the *life* and how he and his father sometimes would park the car in a storm and walk into a field to know how it felt to be "cut off." This "practice" death ("out in the dark alone") prepares him for the reality of death. Then, he could rest secure in the knowledge that he could always go home. Now, he has to face the fact that everyone, himself included, is a tenant on this earth. He accepts the fact of his own "borrowed" breath and, therefore, can "step forward" to learn of his father's death. "Circle of Breath" prepares the reader for many more poems about the poet's father and his influence on the way the poet thinks. The father remains, somehow, the "home" to which the poet turns; the poems recover, briefly, his felt presence, and attest to his persistent influence. "Listening" describes how his father could hear what no one else could hear (animal steps, moths, "every far sound") so that the family relied on him to bring some of that knowledge in to them. With his death, they are left with the legacy of expectation: "My father heard so much that we still stand / inviting the quiet by turning the face, /

waiting for a time when something in the night / will touch us too from that other place" (33, *63*). Listening, not seeing, becomes his method of discovery. From this poem on, the word *listening* is allusive: it represents his father's method of knowing and a goal to which the poet can aspire.

From this remembered place in the center of the country, the book faces west. West becomes not only a direction but a step into time, both the past and the future. "West" is the almost mythological location—the "ultimate wind, the whole land's wave" (29, *60*)—where the wilderness offers a way of being in the world. It is equated with the American psyche. It is the unmapped, and unmappable, territory of lost history and yet-to-be-realized possibilities. The American Indians are a constant presence; "Our People" speaks for the Indians, in the guise of a persona. Stafford has imaginatively entered the history of the Indians, remembering how "our people" stood in the wind in their own "lived story" (36, *65*). To some extent Stafford takes on the task of telling that story. Many of the poems mention Indian legend or call up the lore of the west—imaginative and historical, contemporary and legendary: Billy the Kid, Willa Cather, place names abounding (Yellow Knife, Snake River, Highway 40, Bing Crosby's ranch). By rooting the reader in geography Stafford is able to suggest two levels of meaning; the west is both the real, desirable wilderness and, at the same time, an unattainable state of mind. This attitude, with its accompanying conflict, is clearly exemplified in what might seem like the slightest of poems, "Vacation":

One scene as I bow to pour her coffee:—

> Three Indians in the scouring drouth
> huddle at a grave scooped in the gravel,
> lean to the wind as our train goes by.
> Someone is gone.
> There is dust on everything in Nevada.

I pour the cream. (39, *67*)

In what is a deceptively simple poem Stafford establishes a way of looking at the world. As a couple look out of the window of a train—in the instant between the time he has poured the coffee and the pouring of the cream—a scene is noted. The scene is age-old: drouth, the scooped grave, the bowed heads which lean into the wind. "Someone is gone." The traveler does not know who, cannot share the grief, can only note the stoic ritual of burial and the dust that seems to cover everything. He is the observer, traveling through; they are participating in a ritual that links them to the past, and with the land itself. He can only note, and pour the cream. The pouring (inside) is in apposition (and opposition) to the drouth (outside). His experience of the land, and of the past, can only take place in language. "Scouring," "scooped," "dust" give us the writer's *perceptions*; "bow," "pour," "pour" define the real time—the fraction of a minute in which time hesitates, then rights itself and goes on.

It is important to note that the title of the book includes the reader. "Your" city (as opposed to "my" or "the") insinuates that wherever one lives, there is a territory to the "west"—a vast, unexplored frontier where courage and convictions will be tested. This territory may be literal or figurative; whichever, the journey can only lead to self-knowledge. "Walking West" introduces the solitary walker who inhabits the poems of William Stafford, leaving his individual trail to show that he was here. This poem holds time (and God) still so that anyone, including the reader, can feel the natural forces at work. The distance—"mountains that are far from people"—establishes how removed these forces are from the human scale. They are "forever" (35, 65).

Part of Stafford's "westward" journey led him to encounter his old nemesis—"man's inhumanity to man." War was never far from the national consciousness; it had dominated the youth of Stafford's generation and now, in the late 50s, the Cold War resulted in a national "paranoia." "At the Bomb Testing Site," one of Stafford's most famous poems, uncovers that underlying paranoia and points up its inevitable consequences. Man's inhumanity to man becomes inhumanity to nature. What will become of all who share this planet?

> At noon in the desert a panting lizard
> waited for history, its elbows tense,
> watching the curve of a particular road
> as if something might happen.

It was looking at something farther off
than people could see, an important scene
acted in stone for little selves
at the flute end of consequences.

There was just a continent without much on it
under a sky that never cared less.
Ready for a change, the elbows waited.
The hands gripped hard on the desert. (41, 67)

By giving the lizard elbows and hands, Stafford makes the reader aware that what happens at the bomb testing site will affect him as well. Nature is indifferent—the sky "never cared less"—but people can care. If something is going to "happen," then that something will be a result of human activity and it will affect the world beyond the scope of immediate human ends. The lizard, with its history of change and evolution, knows more about the "flute end of consequences" than people, with their foolish need to dominate the world. The careful understatement of this poem means that its impact is all the more effective. It suggests that if the reader can care about the lizard and his steadfast gripping on the desert, he ought to be able to care about his fellow humans. Stafford will not let us escape the consequences, but he does not hammer his point home. He presents it in a quiet, conversational tone, almost as though he believed that, possibly, something might *not* happen; he implies that if humanity can anticipate, it might survive.

In the center of *West of Your City*, and central to the book, is a longer, six-part poem, "The Move to California." This poem establishes the sweep of the book—the courage it takes to uproot one's family, the way in which the geography of the land mirrors an internal geography; the Great Divide of the soul, so to speak. The move is introduced in almost mystical terms; an "angel of blown newspaper" announces its summons. The speaker suggests that it does no good to question some things ("there are things you cannot learn through manyness"). His own journey is equivalent to the westward expansion of the earlier settlers, but "it takes a lot of miles to equal one wildcat." He settles the land by traveling it and by taking in its details as part of the "measure [of] God's kindness." (44-7, 69-72)

This sense of movement, seen in the explicit places mentioned in "The Move to California," is mirrored internally, as a spiritual move, in "Bi-Focal," whose very title indicates doubleness of vision. A legend is seen to be moving "up out of this land"; it is something "under love." Love is of the surface, for those presently inhabiting the earth, but the fixed legend is more profound—and more enduring. The poem ends on a prophetic note:

> As fire burns the leaf
> and out of the green appears
> the vein in the center line
> and the legend veins under there,
>
> So, the world happens twice—
> once what we see it as;
> second it legends itself
> deep, the way it is. (48, 72)

This duality, the way things seem and the way things are, is central to Stafford's work. For him, the second way of experiencing the world manifests itself in the writing of the poem. There is a moment in which things "happen"—often a moment that is almost unnoticed. Sometimes the transformation seems to take place in language itself, as in "the legend veins under there." This use of *veins* as a verb serves to call attention to the word itself and to suggest other possible meanings and understandings. Most of all, the identification of "legends" with the "way it is" indicates the importance of the poetic act: the land comes alive only in the telling, the imaginative re-creation that opens the world to the listener. This is the motive behind the narrative that underlies almost all of Stafford's poems; they hinge on a story that is working toward the universal. Both story and image are evoked in language, and it is on this level that contact is made. This is explicit in "A Ritual to Read to Each Other": "And so I appeal to a voice, to something shadowy, / a remote important region in all who talk" (52, 75).

Another poem, "Outside," suggests further complexity—that of "a truth greater than ours." The "comfortable" earth is inhabited by animals as well as people, and the poem ends by saying "Coyotes are circling around our truth" (49, 73). They may know more than we do. Stafford implies that it is our duty to be receptive to this larger truth. Several other poems circle around this implication. "I place my feet with care in such a world" (51-2, 75) says the speaker of "The Well Rising." Watching water rise without sound, or swallows in their "swerve" coming closer and closer to this truth, the poet is made aware of the tenuous connections between people. Accident can betray, he says; people may fail to understand each other. He ends "A Ritual to Read to Each Other," clearly a poem about human communication, with "the signals we give—yes or no, or maybe— / should be clear: the darkness around us is deep" (52, 76).

This darkness is reminiscent of an earlier darkness in "The Farm on the Great Plains," a poem in which Stafford imagines phoning home—over time and distance and even death—then coming to a central wisdom: "both ends will be home:/ no space, no birds, no farm" (34, 64). With a "braille eye" (denoting blindness) and a cold telephone line (denoting deafness), the poet's only recourse is to language. He will recapture the farm (and with it his parents) on a night that is, at last, the "right one." "My self will be the plain," the poet says, fusing his past and present lives into one (remembered) location.

"The Farm on the Great Plains" echoes a desire for "home"— the place to call every year. But desire resides wholly in language, emphasizing the irretrievable. The future tense ("I will ring the line" and "my self will be the plain") is only possible in a poem. The past resides in memory, slipping into the present tense of desire. The poet is aware of this; in some sense, he returns only to perfect the loss, "pacing toward what I know" (and will go on knowing—through writing).

"Connections" is a nearly archetypal poem which states "Ours is a low, curst, under-swamp land" (53, 76). From this watery beginning, the poem examines the inter-connections of life on this planet. The raccoon dips his paw into the swamp but cannot find the "thread." The reader also looks under the surface for a larger meaning; it is glimpsed in the close-to-death quality of the sneeze— all-consuming, transitory, illusory ("a sneeze may glimpse us Paradise"). Masks are everywhere. It is difficult to find the larger truth; the road is littered with paradox—technology can kill as well as cure: "And if we purify the pond, the lilies die." The "connections" are fragile, and they must be honored.

By the end of this first poetry volume, Stafford seems to be raising the question of what to make, not of the land, but of the world. There is something, in Stafford's terminology, "underneath" the earth—the ongoing legend of its entire history. The external world gives us glimpses; to enter the myth, one must find a way to travel easily between the external and internal, bridge the gap between the individual and the shared, and find the message that is buried deep. "Level Light" is a typical poem, one that suggests much more than it pretends to be saying:

> Sometimes the light when evening fails
> stains all haystacked country and hills,
> runs the cornrows and clasps the barn
> with that kind of color escaped from corn
> that brings to autumn the winter word—
> a level shaft that tells the world:
>
> > It is too late now for earlier ways;
> > now there are only some other ways,
> > and only one way to find them—fail.
>
> In one stride night then takes the hill. (50, 74)

In this extraordinarily musical poem, the poet has found an answer in the natural world. That answer is to fail (at least in human terms) in order to gain the balance, or levelling, of light. The earth hovers between seasons; we are between "ways." *West of Your City* is groping toward a new "way." And Stafford feels *his* way through sound. The poem is a carefully rhymed piece, teasing the ear with variations in rhythm, assonance, consonance, alliteration, repetition (note the doubly rhymed "fail" and "hill"). The tone, however, is the opposite of formal; Stafford skillfully employs the techniques of formal verse to enhance his informal tone. In living, in poetry, he is searching for something new.

If Stafford surprises the reader with this blend of the formal and informal, he also surprises the reader in his choice of language. "We anticipated something we did not expect" (50). "This river is what tawny is and loneliness" (42). Beneath the surface of language, just as beneath the surface of the ice in "Ice-Fishing," is the "wild flipping warmth of won-back thought" (51, 74). Below the surface of knowledge lies intuition; trusting that intuition may lead to salvation.

In "It Is the Time You Think," Stafford once more enters the realm of the hunted—the deer, the soldier—hoping to ferret out the meaning of one instant before it blends with all other instants, the "little pause before / real things happen." He suggests that he would rather not be one of the "logical ones," though in the end he can't quite divorce himself from them. The "expected act" is contrasted with the "real things" that will happen, because it is surprise that teaches and gives new understanding. Yet Stafford's speaker is also a skeptic:

> I am too local a creature to take the truth
> unless and until by God it happens to me. (55)

3
Some Right Song
Traveling Through the Dark

In 1962 Stafford published the book that won him a national reputation. *Traveling Through the Dark* was chosen for the National Book Award in 1963. Here the themes apparent in his first book recur, adding depth to an already established vision. The poems are filled with familiar images and phrases, but the exploration of these images takes the reader into new territory. The voice in this book is surer, less questioning, but the questions are there, nevertheless. The quietly conversational tone pulls the reader in, the subject matter is fairly straightforward, the poems appear to be accessible. But under the surface, the current is often dangerously deep, and the undertow makes them richly complex.

The title poem, "Traveling Through the Dark," is an example of this mixture of accessibility and complexity. Its form on the page is simple—four four-line stanzas and an ending couplet—and its narrative line is easy to follow. A careful reading, though, unearths the contradictory impulses that make this an important poem:

> Traveling through the dark I found a deer
> dead on the edge of the Wilson River road.
> It is usually best to roll them into the canyon:
> that road is narrow; to swerve might make more
> > dead.
>
> By glow of the tail-light I stumbled back of the car
> and stood by the heap, a doe, a recent killing;
> she had stiffened already, almost cold.
> I dragged her off; she was large in the belly.
>
> My fingers touching her side brought me the
> > reason—
> her side was warm; her fawn lay there waiting,
> alive, still, never to be born.
> Beside that mountain road I hesitated.

> The car aimed ahead its lowered parking lights;
> under the hood purred the steady engine.
> I stood in the glare of the warm exhaust turning red;
> around our group I could hear the wilderness listen.
>
> I thought hard for us all—my only swerving—,
> then pushed her over the edge into the river.[1]

A reading of this poem should serve as a method for studying much of Stafford's work. So many things work simultaneously in the poem that to look at them separately is artificial. But the reading must start somewhere. This particular poem has a strong narrative line, so the first assessment is of the story. A man is driving on a narrow mountain road when he comes upon a dead deer. Without hesitation he stops to do what he considers his duty—roll it over the edge into the canyon. As he leaves his car he has no doubts. But then—the doe has an unborn fawn—suddenly there is (at least for the speaker) a conflict. He is faced with a decision. Could he save the fawn? Should he save it if he could? Very little time is given to the decision in this poem, and yet time hangs heavy with expectation until the final, quick turn when he does as he originally intended. The thought that precedes that action is the subject of this poem, just as it was the triggering impulse for the poem in the first place.

Did this event really happen? Does it come from the writer's life? Those might be the first questions. This cannot be known—or rather, it is not important to know. What is important is that the reader *believe* that it happened. Belief comes easily in this case because Stafford names the road (the Wilson River Road) and because of the easy, conversational tone he adopts ("It is usually best. . ."), which draws the reader into the poem as if to share with its speaker some communal knowledge, a way of doing things. We follow his directions, thinking from inside. The reader experiences the discovery of the deer, and the speaker's dilemma, with somewhat the same emotions as the writer. The speaker conveys a sense of mental agitation; he clearly doesn't want to make the decision by himself. Caught between worlds, he invokes a "group" as though it could be a communal decision—"around our group I could hear the wilderness listen." The group appears to be the man, the deer, the unborn fawn, and, by extension, all of nature. This is understood. But the group also seems to include the car. The car is, very possibly, the most alive thing in this poem. It is active; it "aims its parking lights"; it glows, it is warm, almost breathing. The car (and the human who invented it) is both the instrument of death and representative of life. It is the occupants of other cars that he would be saving on that narrow road. The poem becomes immediately complex by introducing this paradox. The poet's decision is not now so much a matter of the life and death of one particular fawn as of our whole relationship to nature. That the speaker doesn't come to an easy decision is clear; there is hesitation, the hard thoughts, the "swerving." This word takes on weight by virtue of its being used twice. In the first stanza, it is used literally. The second time the word is used, the "swerving" is internal; it takes place in the poet's mind, a mind forever altered because of the decision he has been forced to make. If he got out of the car with confidence, he gets back in full of doubt.

This poem demonstrates the encroachment of mechanized society on the wilderness. It does not so much debate the right or wrong of the speaker's action as raise the questions of what is right and wrong under these conditions. Does one go against nature in order to honor it? Or does one acquiesce to an order larger than one man can devise? An underlying sense of guilt is shown in the progression of the words used to describe the deer— *heap* to *doe* to *killing*—and the ordering of the words surrounding the fawn—*alive, still* (still alive?), *never to be born* (stillborn?). "Around our group I could *hear* the wilderness *listen*." There's a doubled listening—man and nature attentive to each other, each with something to offer, something to take. To listen to the act of listening is to be answered by silence.

This poem is a frame of mind, and part of its unsettled quality can be found in its rhymes. At first glance it does not appear to have rhymes. But an examination of the second and fourth lines of each stanza shows that *road* and *dead* are both one-syllable words ending in *d*. *Killing* and *belly* have two syllables each, with the double *l* in the center of each word. *Waiting* and *hesitated* share the long *a* and are similar in meaning. *Engine* and *listen* reverse their vowel sounds but share the *n* humming through them. *Swerving* and *river* not only have the central *v* in common, but the *er* sound. This slant rhyme suggests a lack of resolution, a feeling of "near miss." Stafford embodies his doubts as they are mirrored in sounds too close to be accidental but too different to be lulling.

What was originally merely a title that gives a set of circumstances—a man at night in his car—now gives much more. This journey is through the darkness of indecision, doubt, death. It is allegorical. Does he come out at the other side into light? The poem suggests that Stafford is still groping with the questions that the poem raises; it does not offer up easy answers. In fact, the unanswered questions add to, and are part of, its "darkness." When questioned about this poem in an interview with Sanford Pinsker, Stafford said, "Choices are always Hobson's choices. All you have to do is get a little more alert to see that even your best moves are compromises—and complicated."[2] This shows a man aware of what his action (or his poem) did not do, as well as what it did.

The slant rhymes, the rhythm, the cadence, all demonstrate what Stafford describes as one of the forces playing on the writer. "You are always modulating along in sound. The writer and the speaker always live in one big chime."[3] It is this part of Stafford—the part receptive to the chime—that made him choose to say "deer / dead" rather than "dead / deer" in the first stanza. He was attuned to the developing slant rhymes, and to the life-affirming opening line, which then turns toward tragedy by the first word of the second.

Traveling Through the Dark helps to clarify the stance of the poet. In the title poem, Stafford's speaker is an involved participant, but the poem is rendered in the past tense, so that from the beginning the speaker is distanced from the act or the thought, able to assess and comment on his actions. Because of its simple language, the presence of the poet is not felt by the reader. This distance, which allows the poet to act as observer, is characteristic. In this way the poet can serve as a witness. There is a sense of otherness, even when the poem is told in the first-person singular. Sometimes this distance is the distance of memory—distorted, imperfect, locked in the past—and sometimes it is the distance that must be covered by the imagination in order to enter the lives or experiences of others. This is seen in the poem, "Thinking for Berky." The title itself surprises—how does one think *for*, rather than *of* or *about*? The poem begins with the speaker lying in bed, listening to an ambulance, thinking . . .

> In the late night listening from bed
> I have joined the ambulance or the patrol
> screaming toward some drama, the kind of end
> that Berky must have some day, if she isn't dead (64,
>   *80*).

What follows is memory—the recollection of a girl who had no chance, whose earliest experiences were of cruelty and abuse. Berky represents that part of society that is living on the edge. She wants, and needs, to be rescued but has no power to save herself. The speaker says, "Windiest nights, Berky, I have thought for you, / and no matter how lucky I've been I've touched wood." He feels "lucky," knowing that under the surface of his luck lies her misfortune. Out of this comes a sense of responsibility— responsibility to think for her since she can't think for herself and also to think *for* her by committing himself to her. This sends him not only back into the past but forward, into the future he predicts for Berky:

> There are things not solved in our town though
>   tomorrow came:
> there are things time passing can never make come
>   true.

These lines, hinged by the colon that would try to equate them, are examples of how time, for Stafford, does not exist in a linear fashion. First he talks from the future looking back and then from the past looking forward.

In most Stafford poems there seems to be a line that asks more questions than the rest of the poem can answer. The final stanza begins: "We live in an occupied country, misunderstood." Suddenly the pronoun ("we") includes the reader as well as the speaker and Berky. Who, one asks, is occupied, is occupying? "Justice will take us millions of intricate moves." He accepts that it may be too late for Berky, that justice will come slowly, after many small steps. The poet locates himself in the middle of "us," trying to make us realize that many small moves do add up to real change. The poet has become a witness for a certain point of view, and he has done this by moving from the particular to the general, from the real past to an imagined future. Meanwhile, the poem is relentless: "Sirens will hunt down Berky, you survivors in your beds." Everyone is implicated in her fate, unsettled, awakened by the sirens that signify a flawed society.

In *Traveling through the Dark*, Stafford not only speaks eloquently for the remembered people of his past, demonstrating his ongoing concern for the underdog, but he also begins to speak more generally for the whole of society. The pronouns *we* and *our* proliferate. Many of the poems take on a timeless quality, as though spoken by a sage, by someone who has observed for centuries: "These mountains have heard God" ("The Tillamook Burn," 73, *84-5*); "Summer will rise till the houses fear" ("Summer Will Rise," 85); "A storm that needed a mountain / met it where we were" ("Found in a Storm," 102, *99*). Others seem to speak directly to the reader, carrying an oracular authority: "Imagine a voice calling" ("From the Gradual Grass," 98); "Think of a river beyond your thought" ("Interlude," 105). Still others speak intimately to a remembered "you" who comes alive in the poem, a presence behind it. Each of these techniques serves to create a slight distance between poet and reader, between poet and poem. In this space, Stafford's guiding sensibility is allowed free rein.

Part of this sensibility, in spite of the gravity of the issues it confronts and the sincerity with which it confronts them, is a lack of pomposity or self-importance. Stafford's characteristic stance toward himself is wry, often ironic, as when he compares himself to his father: ". . .preferring to be saved and not, like him, heroic." He mocks his own limitations even while he acknowledges them: "I want to be as afraid as the teeth are big, / I want to be as dumb as the wise are wrong" ("Parentage," 67, *82*). There is a gentle humor running through these poems which is reassuring; the speaker does not set himself above anyone. Sometimes there is a shared recognition of the truth behind the humor: "Some people you meet are so dull / that you always remember their names" ("The Trip," 96, *96*). Yet Stafford is not harsh in his judgments, probably because he includes himself in each of them.

Stafford's inclination to slip between past and future, as well as within time and space, is evident in *Traveling Through the Dark*. "My father was ahead in shadows, my son / behind coming into the streetlight" ("*In Medias Res*," 61, *78*). "We were traveling between a mountain and Thursday" ("Holding the Sky," 68). This slippage allows him room for exploration. He places himself squarely in the middle of things and twists in the wind, letting language itself decide where he will settle. The writing begins to take more and more the form of listening. *Listen* is used often and is a key word in Stafford's poems, as though the act of listening can get it "right" in ways the act of writing can only approximate. Writing sounds too much like knowing, while listening is closer to understanding. The Stafford stance—dead center in the poem, and in society—is one of articulating a shared knowledge.

Another recurring word in *Traveling Through the Dark* is *fear.* There is the fear of death, as seen in the title poem, and the accompanying greater fear of making a wrong decision. In fact, Stafford seems to give license to fear, making it an acceptable emotion for anyone to have. To admit it might be to tame it. But the fear seems, in the end, to be nameless—and pervasive. The image is often one of glancing backward, of being taken unexpectedly by something. Words such as *danger, worry, terrible, separate,* and *change* predominate. It is as if he is afraid of not knowing. "Late at Night" suggests that the geese, in their inexorable flight, have a kind of knowledge that people wish for, and can never hope to approximate (86, 92). "Fall Wind," which blends both the sense of listening and the sense of fear, is exemplary of this attitude:

> Pods of summer crowd around the door;
> I take them in the autumn of my hands.
>
> Last night I heard the first cold wind outside;
> the wind blew soft, and yet I shiver twice:
>
> Once for thin walls, once for the sound of time. (95,
>   95)

Again Stafford exhibits his double sense of the world—the thin walls of his own room and a second, deeper sense of the thin walls of centuries. The premonition is completed on the second, more abstract, level, and the poet is left with nowhere to look but toward his knowledge of death ("autumn hands"). This other realm is mirrored in another poem, "Requiem," where the ongoing earthly details (bird song, rocks clinking, locusts, moss) exist simultaneously with the fact of his mother's death; now she is traveling "north" to become part of the flow of time, the "rites of yesterday." This concept of death as a fusion with all that is natural is at the heart of Stafford's poetry. At the end of the poem the speaker says, "Our duty is just a certain high kind of waiting" (8). This waiting (while life unfolds) is more intense due to this sense of duty. Death—both his own and that of others—is earned through the lived life. Thus, at the root of this book is a quest for how to live.

Stafford's prescription is complicated. "Lake Chelan" calls on a hypothetical man ("someone like a trapper's child" 84, *91*) in a distant city to discover a lake and all of its history within his imagination. The poem urges an embodiment of the wilderness in the "deepest place we have." Here Stafford plainly refutes the critics who would call his work regional. The region that he claims is internal; it contains a "model of our land," the lonely place from which people speak. To find an equivalent in that larger world where gravity determines the level of the lake is to find oneself. The self one finds in this manner is secure in its knowledge. It can "represent" those "far places" in the imagination. As in "Representing Far Places," it is so in touch with the natural world that "witty" talk at a party only reinforces the sense of isolation. It has earned the right to say "it is all right to be simply the way you have to be" (97, *97*). This realization gives Stafford *permission* to write. "He searches for some right song / that could catch and then shake the world, / any night by the steady stove," says the speaker of "Late Thinker" (104). The "right song" may be the poem with its accompanying messages for how to live. And poems are made by listening hard, discovering the "far places" where poems originate or have validity. This is also seen in "'The Lyf so Short'." Echoing Chaucer, this poem looks at the poet's life in "that room larger than the world"—imagination—where we are "forced backward into our dreams." The final stanza moves from the past into the present:

> Today we have to stand in absolute rain
> and face whatever comes from God,
> or stoop to smooth the earth over little things
> that went into dirt, out of the world. (89, *93*)

The only place to hold things that have gone "out of the world" is in memory, and memory is imbued with a sense of the ideal. Locked in the past, people and places are perfected. This is never more evident than in one of Stafford's most important poems, "In Dear Detail, by Ideal Light." Its first section begins:

> Night huddled our town,
> plunged from the sky.
> You moved away.
> I save what I can of the time. (105, *100*)

The poem goes on to ask: "Can we rescue the light / that happened, and keeps on happening, around us?" He remembers someone (a "you") who was left there "surrounded by the river curve" (the flow of time) and now surfaces like "vision emergencies . . . coming near at unlikely places." The second section deals with the "duty" to find a place in the world even if it means leaving others behind. From the vantage point of a secure place in the world, it is possible to give memory its head, allowing memory to "rescue" the past:

> There, for the rest of the years,
> by not going there, a person could believe
> some porch looking south,
> and steady in the shade—maybe you,
>
> Rescued by how the hills
> happened to arrive where they are,
> depending on that wire
> going to an imagined place
>
> Where finally the way the world feels
> really means how things are,
> in dear detail,
> in ideal light all around us. (106, *101*)

"*Maybe* you." The uncertainty is there in the choice of that word, in words like *happened* and *depending*. The "you" of this poem seems to be a fusion of mother, father, possibly brother and sister, maybe even friends. What is felt is the loss, not of a particular person, but of many "good people," and the tension between the desire to resurrect the past and the impulse to go forward in a diminished world hovers behind the poem. It resolves itself in the final stanza by allowing what "feels" to be what "is." This may be Stafford's version of Stevens's "Let be be finale of seem."[4]

4

Witness

The Rescued Year, Allegiances, and Someday, Maybe

The Rescued Year

The Rescued Year was published by Harper and Row in 1966. Fourteen of the poems had already appeared in the first, limited edition of *West of Your City* and seven had been part of his Ph.D. thesis, "Winterward." Others were written concurrently with the poems in both his first and second volumes. The book demonstrates the consistency of Stafford's vision and Stafford himself feels that *The Rescued Year* is his most unified volume. In a different order, surrounded by other poems, the earlier poems find a new home. By rediscovering these poems in this volume, the serious reader of Stafford is able to identify poems that clearly have importance for the poet, and also to analyze how they function in their new surroundings. Many of the poems that resurface here are poems already noted in *West of Your City* as identifying some of his central concerns. The themes of travel and home, motion and stasis, the duality of vision, the sense of a current beneath the current, all appear. Some key poems that were reprinted in this book include: "One Home," "Vacation," "Listening," "The Well Rising," "At the Bomb Testing Site," "Connections," "Our People," "Bi-Focal," "Ice-Fishing," and "The Move to California."

It is necessary to reassess some of these poems, knowing that they represent what Stafford himself wanted to keep in print. "Ice-Fishing," for example, takes on added importance in its new setting. Surrounded by other poems about water, especially still water (lakes) and stilled water (frozen lakes), "Ice-Fishing" emphasizes the intuitive:

> Not thinking other than how the hand works
> I wait until dark here on the cold
> world rind, ice-curved over simplest rock,

> where the tugged river flows over hidden
> springs too insidious to be quite forgotten.[1]

Again, there is the river and the hidden current—the sense of possible danger (reminiscent of the muskrat in "Ceremony") as well as the source of life. The poem goes on to talk about plunging that hand into the water and bringing up the string of fish as "a great sunburst event."

> . . .and slow
> home with me over unmarked snow
>
> In the wild flipping warmth of won-back thought
> my boots, my hat, my body go.

By the end of the poem, this intuitive trust in the body and its rhythms becomes a statement about poetry and its own travel over "unmarked snow" (blank paper) and the "wild flipping warmth" of natural expression, the last stretch toward "home."

It is also important to examine the new poems in this volume both for their own importance and for ways in which they speak to the earlier work. "The Rescued Year" is a wonderful, far-reaching poem in which Stafford remembers a year spent near the Colorado border—the year his sister "gracefully / grew up." The virtues of that year are enumerated: there were books in the library that they hadn't yet read; school seemed normal, even happy; church was ubiquitous. Stafford then remembers his father's "level gaze" and the way he was taught to appreciate the world. He recalls the little pleasures—making paper presents at Christmas time, the popcorn on the stove in the house of a girlfriend—and, above all, his father's stories. He identifies completely with the father he remembers, emulating his ability to "listen." The final stanza, though, moves the poem from the realm of nostalgia to the realm of recovery:

> In all his ways I hold that rescued year—
> comes that smoke like love into the broken
> coal, that forms to chunks again and lies
> in the earth again in its dim folds, and comes a
>   sound,
> then shapes to make a whistle fade,
> and in the quiet I hold no need, no hurry:

> any day the dust will move, maybe settle;
> the train that left will roll back into our station,
> the name carved on the platform unfill with rain,
> and the sound that followed the couplings back
> will ripple forward and hold the train. (118, *109*)

Stafford imagines everything undone so that it can happen all over again—this time in memory, where hindsight, and language, can rescue or "hold" it. The smoke becomes fire becomes coal becomes earth and all things are reduced to their origins, including a year that bears recovery because they all shared a "treasured unimportance." The reader cannot ignore this desire to be truly unimportant (almost to disappear); that state, for Stafford, allows the poems to begin.

The Rescued Year contains a poem called "Across Kansas" which, despite its title, is anything but a "landscape" poem. Ostensibly, it tells of driving through the night while the family was sleeping. Driving past the town where he was born, the poet says, "I drove down an aisle of sound" (114, *105*), evoking a sense that, for him, (as at the end of "The Rescued Year"), memory and reality reside in sound. The morning light reveals a "self" in everything; the land seems to name itself, the speaker "owns" his face more. But this, too, is a poem about "traveling through the dark," and the final line suggests that even the simple act of driving across his native state is fuel for the poetic imagination: "My state still dark, my dream too long to tell." The landscape is internal. The state is literal and figurative, and so is the darkness. In fact, darkness, where things cannot be seen, is often seen as a necessary condition for imagination or the dream. Stafford continues here to use words in an emblematic way. In addition, the reader notices many words that are repeated (*dream* and *tell* are examples), either resonating throughout this book or recognized from the earlier books. The dream in this instance is the shared dream of writer and something larger—a life force—which sustains everything. "My" dream and the world's dream have, briefly, coincided in that bell of reality, the poem.

By understanding the way key words accumulate to create concentric circles of meaning, the reader finds himself holding the key for unlocking Stafford's poetry. For instance, "Right Now" talks about a secret town where "wires are down" (139). Stafford often mentions wires and the telephone as a means of communication, and often the "long distance" call is difficult to understand, coming, as it does, from the distance of time as well as space. The downed wires and loose connections halt time in this poem. A still wind is blowing the streetlights. A deaf dog is listening. The impossible is possible. "Frozen in this moment," the speaker of the poem is led into his interior darkness where the present is held so perfectly before him he can glimpse, in the stasis, the wildness that is his vision of the times. The poem is despairing, but even more so when the reader understands how the "wires" of the second line resonate with other poems to demonstrate the source of the desperation—the human inability to "connect." On the other hand, out of the particular darkness in this poem comes a moment of self-revelation. A certain kind of connection—speaker with self—has been made.

The Rescued Year features a long series of poems, loosely pulled together under the title "Following the *Markings* of Dag Hammarskjöld: A Gathering of Poems in the Spirit of His Life and Writings." The landscape of these poems is bleak, basically Godless, as best demonstrated in the final poem, "Walking the Wilderness." God, if there is one, is found in the power of the elements, especially the dark and the cold (each snowflake is God's answer—with its individual design and their collective pattern). God is simply there, unaware of opposition; indifference characterizes His attitude toward humans. But humans are "dignified" by the elements, in this case the "last" blizzard, and the end of the poem suggests that, in a spirit of ultimate recognition, we should hold out to God "no trembling hand" (138). Stafford's later discussion of religion, "The Poet as Religious Moralist," reprinted in *You Must Revise Your Life*, reveals his attitude: "My sense of the nature of God is neither firm nor infirm; it is just there. . . . My belief is just something like where north is to a compass: I can sway; I can be confused. But north is still there."[2]

"North" often functions in this way—less as a direction and more as an indicator of the presence of God or of a natural force which humans cannot alter. So, too, the words *cold* and *sky* become part of Stafford's representation of God—the endless, persistent otherness of things outside the human consciousness. The final image of this sequence accepts that man (the "walker") will meet God ("blizzard" weds the elements, the cold, and the sky) on equal terms, bringing to death his own sense of the "deep of that dream."

This sequence of poems also illustrates the way Stafford's work constantly moves outward in order to speak for more than just himself. His imaginative entry into the sensibility of Hammarskjöld is an act of homage; the older poet and statesman becomes a father-figure. But Stafford also speaks for the oppressed and the endangered. In "The Concealment: Ishi, the Last Wild Indian," Ishi is resurrected to force a comparison between old and new. The inhabitants of California are characterized as his "opposites"—with all the moral judgment this implies. "It was all right / for him to make a track" (136, *117*). Each individual life counts in the longer dream that the world is telling.

Four other poems in this volume bear mentioning. The first is an antiwar poem which is startling in its surprise ending. Called "The Epitaph Ending in And," this poem startles first by assuming that the end is inevitable (it is not called "*An* Epitaph. . ."). The poem assumes the reader is familiar with what happens in an atomic explosion:

> In the last storm, when hawks
> blast upward and a dove is
> driven into the grass, its broken wings
> a delicate design, the air between
> wracked thin where it stretched before,
> a clear spring bent close too often
> (that Earth should ever have such wings
> burnt on in blind color!), this will be
> good as an epitaph:
>
> Doves did not know where to fly, and (127, *114*)

The sentence, cut off at mid-point, reminds us that doves, eternal symbol of peace, are not all that will be destroyed.

The second introduces a new strain in his work—the writer as teacher. "At This Point on the Page" poignantly describes a teacher's realization that his pupil's writing represents something painful, and hard won, for the student. The teacher does not want to go on reading, at least not "by prose" (130, *115*), suggesting that there is some territory that can only be dealt with in poetry, in that feeling *toward* something important in the shared experience of writer and reader.

The third is a poem about poetry itself that has been widely quoted and which does seem to represent Stafford's quirky view of what poetry is and what it can do. "Walking along in this not quite prose way" (144, *117*) is the opening line of "Near," and in that line, Stafford establishes that poetry has a rhythm and, possibly, a vision of its own. He goes on to say "it is time to notice this intolerable snow / innumerably touching" as though to demonstrate the possibilities for sound that prose cannot quite produce. This poem reinforces the idea that listening becomes a metaphorical way of being receptive to nature, and to the process of creating art. Stafford uses sound instead of sight when he wants to learn something new. Since the writing of poetry is, for him, an exploration into new territory, by extension his use of this word signals that the poem is forming: "listen—it is falling not quite silently / and under it still you and I are walking." Poet and reader, self and other, the shared experience is one of *sound*. Sound for Stafford often follows Frost's prescription for a "sentence sound."[3] For Stafford the basic unit is a sentence; the lines break across it, giving it a fresh look. Commas connect seemingly dissociated ideas, gluing the various pieces together to make a complicated pattern, rich with layers.

The fourth new poem is essential for understanding all previous and later work. Entitled "Across the Lake's Eye" (141), this poem reinforces the concept of water as all that contains depth (that which is knowable but unseeable). And yet here it is the lake that seems to "see." Walking over what is frozen to the edge of deep water, the speaker of the poem and his companion are able to see other worlds (stars reflected in dark water). The seeing is double-edged; the speaker can look in two directions, plumbing the depths, and the lake itself can reflect sky (and even the light of now extinct stars) while it holds its own watery secrets. Below, there is "a left-hand world," says the companion (who may just possibly be the true double, the alter-ego of the poet), a "negative of the world." Then the left-hand story is spun about an island that rose from under the water and pretended to be other than the one it was. "Sound is dead there, but haunts the concave water / where the island used to be." Poetry, the poem suggests, can only represent what is true, cannot create something other than what chimes with the larger, natural world. The two walk homeward, leaving their own trail in the snow as further evidence of this discovery.

Allegiances

Allegiances was published in 1970. This book is vintage Stafford, but a Stafford who had become familiar; some of the poems feel as though they had been read before. Possibly for this reason critics and scholars began to call for more rigor, for an editorial decision on Stafford's part to publish only what is truly "good." Stafford was steadfast in refusing to make that critical decision, preferring to let the reader discover what he will. He left the judging to those he termed the "logical ones." His consistent stance was that each poem is a discovery, that it has its own place, however slight, and that he was unwilling to cut himself off from the wellspring of poetry by exercising too rational a judgment on his own work. Readers have no choice but to follow his direction and to decide for themselves which poems will survive the test of time. Since Stafford hardly seemed to be writing for fame and fortune, scholarly opinion did not matter as much to him as his own sense of authenticity.

Allegiances proves what can be inferred from the earlier volumes. The influence of family is reasserted; there are poems about his father, mother, brother. "Home" is again seen to represent the self, an idealized, irretrievable self. The landscape of the book is rural—plains, farm, home—and the context in which these occur is that of memory. What began to be evident in *West of Your City* is confirmed here; place is an informing spirit more than a real, physical setting. Home is where the heart is, where the individual life can best yield up material for the poetic impulse to nurture.

The "allegiances" that Stafford feels are to people and place; several of the poems refer to places in Kansas or people from the past, especially those who cannot speak for themselves. Some show allegiance to animals (usually wolves, coyotes, owls—animals of the night), who "hurt no one" (185). Others are to an idealized history where "the past, its wisdom" is "quick in the head again" (190)—alive in memory. Still others have their allegiance to ideas or ideals. The ideal, as seen in this volume, is to be found in the ordinary. Stafford calls himself one of the "common ones" and hopes in "Allegiances" that "we ordinary beings can cling to the earth and love / where we are, sturdy for common things" (193, *129*). In this volume, more than in many of the others, small poems make the reader look at common objects or natural phenomena— tree, flower, field, wind, light, time. These things function and have importance in Stafford's world. "Earth Dweller," a poem that could be called "transcendental," shows this well. The overheard speaker stands on a farm and everything seems suddenly precious, even the crack in the axe handle. For an instant, he is at one with the universe:

> somewhere inside, the clods are
> vaulted mansions, lines through the barn sing
> for the saints forever. (196, *129*)

But Stafford comes back to the earth; the transformation is completed in the real world and is even undercut by the questioning sensibility that says, "If I have not found the right place, / teach me."

To some it may seem that the clarity of vision that characterized the earlier work is not to be found in *Allegiances*. The focus has blurred. The consistent voice and the unique angle of vision persist, but the deep connection between his internal and his external life seems to have broken down. The underlying *tension* is gone. The poems (and the volume) lack a felt conviction. Yet they fit easily into the larger direction that one senses underneath the body of his work. How does one assess these poems? This problem is magnified with a writer like Stafford, who states that he is not attempting to shape each poem as a finite object and that success and failure are not an issue.

One poem about being with his daughter begins by looking forward rather than back, providing a sense of continuity and parental commitment. "With Kit, Age 7, at the Beach" is a simple story of looking out to the ocean after a climb over the dunes. His daughter asks how far he could swim. Knowing that the waves stretch forever, that they are "far, and cold," he is also aware that the question holds implications as to what he would do to save her. "As far as was needed," he answers, mentally swimming, braving any storm for her (152, *120*). The instant wisdom of the father, the depth of his emotion, the intense desire to be everything the child will need, are recognizable—and endearing. The poems are on a human scale. They ask only that we experience the world as it is.

But 1970 saw a nation caught up in the Vietnam War. That was the year of the bombings in Cambodia and the shooting at Kent State. Stafford's poems do not allow the reader to forget. They mention Martin Luther King, Governor Wallace, exploding bombs. In the first stanza of "Evening News," he demonstrates this social consciousness; for Stafford it is impossible to ignore the environment in which he lives:

> That one great window puts forth
> its own scene, the whole world
> alive in glass. In it a war happens,
> only an eighth of an inch thick. (183)

The war may seem unreal, television thin, but he has lost friends to this war, and so he goes out to check on his yard, to see if the world he knows and loves might still be there. He "prays" that birds, wind, "unscheduled" grass (as opposed to the kind planted on graves) will make things "go deep again." The nation has lost its sense of purpose, and Stafford reflects its troubled times.

The very lack of overt antiwar poems suggests that the national problems were overwhelming for Stafford, a man who could be expected to have strong opinions and to write them eloquently. *Allegiances* may be quietly revolutionary in its insistence that we pay attention to the world. In a year that saw Lowell's *Notebook* published, a year in which the country had become self-conscious to the point of confusion, Stafford was quietly urging us not to lose balance. He seems to be saying: The earth is still here, "justice will take us millions of intricate moves," keep going, steadily. Like *Walden*, it simultaneously offers us an exhortation to duty and a process for healing.

"In Sublette's Barn" best exemplifies this attitude. Sublette, a "reluctant hero," moved into the wilderness ("once that place / was found, The West had come, no one could undiscover it," 158). Sublette's story as recounted in the poem is not heroic; it is the story of a man who "listened to the current" and followed where it led. He learned to respond to the land until the land seemed to hold his spirit. The land "meant" him. Our work, then, the poem states, is to forget the wilderness in order to go forth into it. Earth's the right place for love,[4] the book suggests; "it is our only friend" (196, *129*). But "So Long," the final poem of *Allegiances*, ends with the lonely human knowledge:

> all that we'll have
> to love may be what's near
> in the cold, even then. (198, *131*)

Someday, Maybe

The hesitancy of the title, its refusal to be pinned down or made exact, carries over into the poetry. This book begins on an almost defensive note, as though the comments of the critics had, in fact, had some effect:

> Look: no one ever promised for sure
> that we would sing. We have decided
> to moan. (201, *131*)

It was no longer possible to sing. The nation had only recently looked into the mirrors of My Lai and Watergate. The answer, for the poet who must go on writing in spite of his personal doubt, is to dip into the deep well of language to see if that will yield something in which he can believe. "The authentic is a line from one thing / along to the next." It is as if Stafford's world has been shaken and he needs to know it is still there. Poetry—that body of sound into which he plunges—is his only proof. "Things that say clear, linger: / exact sounds mean the world is there" (208).

In his quest for meaning Stafford devotes a large section of *Someday, Maybe* to Indian stories and legend. He seems to be looking to those original inhabitants for some way to live in peace with the natural world, especially the American experience of it. These are "Stories to Live in the World With," to borrow one of his titles; they add dimension and give perspective. Under the earth, he states, there is "a shock of steadiness" (231).

With hindsight Stafford describes his reaction to the turbulence of the late 1960s and early 70s. He was characteristically reluctant to turn his poetry into a political statement. "Another little quirk isolated me, a reluctance to put my writing to work for any cause," he states. He goes on to say, "When I looked at my writing, though, it proved to be full of issues, positions, and attempted wisdom."[5] These are the poems that readers respond to, partially, one suspects, because Stafford was unable to repress his deepest concerns. One poem, highly reminiscent of the lizard at the bomb testing site, is called "Crossing the Desert":

> Little animals call
> us, tiny feet whisper, and
> a certain wide wing shadow
> flickers down the gray wind
> over the sage.
>
> Pardon! Pardon!—
> a ditch at night is a church
> where eyes burn candles, mile after
> silent mile, whatever comes,
> whatever comes.
>
> Every time the world comes
> true, they cry from the ditch,
> our cousins offering their paws,
> a light hanging in their eyes,
> returning our own. (234)

Here, too, the animal world and the human world are equated; he relates them as closely as "cousins." The wing shadow, with its accompanying threat, ends the first stanza. "Whatever comes" ends the second, and the linkage is made. The repetition of the phrase makes it ominous; whatever it is, it will probably be disastrous. The eyes that glow in the ditches, reflected from the headlights of those who are crossing the desert, become the candles in a church; a prayer for pardon is being offered. The inhabitants of the car are witness to the animals' presence—and to the fragility of their world. As in so many of Stafford's poems, humans are apprehended in the steady gaze of the animals who, while they do not condemn, nevertheless must feel some apprehension. This poem is immediately followed by another yet more ominous,

"After That Sound, After That Sight." The warning must be heeded. One feels the urgency in this pairing of poems:

> After that sound we weren't people
> any more. It came in the night.
> It froze all other sound. We are
> afraid to listen any more.
> After that sight there was hurt
> in every eye. Animals have
> that look, a memory that seeing
> will never make fade.
>
> I walk the world; the day
> falls warm, then thinned.
> Whatever we passed, a sky
> out there swallowed our sky.
> From somewhere else began
> a new part of time. (235)

This is a poem of the apocalypse. A sound and a sight have altered the world forever. One can only imagine the ultimate bomb—the blinding flash and the sound that stops us from being "people any more." This works in two directions; people are destroyed and people, when they act as destroyers, are no longer human. There may be another world, another sky, another time, but life on earth has been permanently altered. There is no possibility of innocence. Poetry does not have the power to prevent, nor to heal. "It froze all other sound."

The last section of *Someday, Maybe* is entitled "Report from a Far Place." Far places figure often in Stafford's work; they represent the source of the poem, the distances of memory, the realm of the imagination. At this point he has stepped into that far territory and is sending back a report. Two important poems dominate this section. "The Swerve" is an account of the death of Stafford's father, probably the fourth such account in the collected work to date. Here there is a finality of tone, as though Stafford can at last make his peace. The title uses one of Stafford's key words—*swerve*—to show that this is not merely a physical swerving but a mental one. His father's car "goes blind" but he was able to steer across the bridge with a light he had "in mind." Here the father, always associated with "listening," is blinded. His death is implied. But the mind can conquer physical loss. The father's mind and the poet's mind meet in the "far place"; the result is a final stanza that seems to make its own prayer:

> Halfway across a bridge one night
> my father's car went blind. He guided
> it on by no star but a light he kept in mind.
>
> Halfway to here, my father died.
> He looked at me. He closed his eyes.
> The world stayed still. Today, I hold in mind
>
> The things he said, my children's lives—
> any light. Oh, any light. (238, *141*)

The short sentences that comprise the second stanza demonstrate the speaker's realization of the finality of death. "My father died." There is no metaphor for this acceptance. "The world stayed still." Time stopped. But the world *still stayed*—dependable, spinning as usual. The children's lives place this death in the larger, on-going cycle of time.

From his vantage in the far place, Stafford is able to explore some of his philosophies, mostly his theory of writing:

> Freedom is not following a river.
> Freedom is following a river,
> though, if you want to. (239)

In "Report from a Far Place," he refers to "these word things" as "snowshoes" (239, *142*). Writing is, for him, like crossing an unbroken field of snow; the reader is expected to follow the tracks.

"Witness" is another central poem. Its title signals its importance; *witness* has become another charged word, a quiet, but specific, testimony. The opening lines are dramatic:

> This is the hand I dipped in the Missouri
> above Council Bluffs and found the springs. (242,
> *144*)

The hand for Stafford is the symbol of service and of love. His own hands worked the sugar beet fields, fought the forest fires.

Throughout his poetry they reach out to touch someone, to take someone into confidence or shared experience. In this poem, the hand has known water, wind, earth. It has saved children and has served as a "diplomat." The speaker trusts that his hand will recognize what is good. The final lines of the poem take the reader to judgment day:

> Even on the last morning
> when we all tremble and lose, I will reach
> carefully, eagerly through that rain, at the end—
>
> Toward whatever is there, with this loyal hand.

The poem ends on a note of faith. "Whatever is there" will be something to which the poet can consign his body eagerly.

The poems in these three "middle" books have much in common. The threat of nuclear war informed much of Stafford's work during this period, manifesting itself in the depiction of a fragile world and a sense of personal vulnerability. Facing this personal fear, Stafford is able to empathize with the situation of others. Many of the poems in these volumes show a sympathy with the "little" people of the world. The poems bear witness *to* injustice, both present and historical. Stafford is a witness *for* alternatives—for values, a way of thinking as well as a way of living. Finally, the poems become quietly religious in a nontraditional sense of that word. In *Allegiances*, the reader is directed, full circle, back to the initial poem in the collection and the "line" that "holds / together something more than the world" (201, 132). The imagination is the key to a collective understanding; "And we are your wavery / efforts at following it." *We* here refers to the poems themselves. And Stafford invites the reader to follow the line into the "wilderness" of the imagination. Are you coming? he asks, are you ready for what I have to offer? If not now, then someday, maybe.

5

What the River Says

Stories That Could Be True and
Things That Happen Where There Aren't Any People

Stories That Could Be True

When *Stories That Could Be True: New and Collected Poems* came out in 1977, it was possible to see William Stafford's work to date as a whole. As a collection of books, it had several threads running through it: nature, people remembered, people observed, home and family, the history of the nation, the history of religion. They were linked, loosely, by the one sensibility that perceived and incorporated them. The pattern was consistent; each section of each book dealt, in some way, with all these themes while emphasizing or highlighting a central concern.

The collected poems were important for scholars who now had the opportunity to see the scope of Stafford's work. Its significance as a collection was immediately recognized. But the new poems in this volume turn in an exciting direction. One section is called "Learning to Live in the World"—signalling the speaker's return from that "far place" to center himself in the present.

To live in the world one must have belief, and the first section of *Stories That Could Be True* is called "Believing." For Stafford the story is paramount. It is the written chronicle of the imagination; it contains all possibilities. He had looked hard at the stories of the American Indians, had "listened" for the stories of people and things, and now he begins building the basis for living in the real world. "Remind me again," he begins "Our Story," talking directly to someone (and to the reader). The poem is inclusive. There is no way to read it without being centered in its direct address. "Some time we'll cross where life / ends."[1] The poem takes poet and reader to the edge of death. Then it ends with a repetition: "Remind me again." The fact of death is something we live with every day, but, the poem reminds us, it is something of which we need to be made aware.

William Stafford's growing awareness of his own eventual death is foreshadowed in *Stories That Could Be True*. "One of Your Lives" dramatizes this: "imagination / left behind by blurred, actual cold / exploding inside your body" (18). The speaker tries to recover the "distance of terror," reaching out to touch a cold face with the growing awareness that it is his own death he is approaching. With this growing acceptance comes a fierce holding to the present, seen in two short poems that capture the moment in very different ways:

> Guitar string is.
> Everything else can wait.
> Silence puts a paw
> wherever the music rests.
>
> All we have is need.
> Before and After are falling.
> Now is going away.
> Sound is the only sky.
>
> Guitar string is:
> it can save this place. (11)

The title of the poem, "Song Now," demonstrates how fleeting the moment is, and how solidly he would like to capture it. The music of the moment predominates. "Guitar string is." The reader listens. It fills the space with its presence and its insistence on the *now*. There is no "before" or "after" when one is caught up in the listening. Even "now" goes away, slipping underneath the insistence of music. The music can save—if not time, then place.

The second poem, "At the Playground," also looks at the moment:

> Away down deep and away up high,
> a swing drops you into the sky.
> Back, it draws you away down deep,
> forth, it flings you in a sweep
> all the way to the stars and back
> —Goodby, Jill: Goodby, Jack:
> shuddering climb wild and steep,
> away up high, away down deep. (11, *53*)

This poem presents the moment in all its fullness, much as the child experiences the timelessness of childhood, the intensity of the lived moment while swinging. It echoes the rhyme and rhythm of the nursery rhyme where the child lives inside the dome of sound. It even refers to Jack and Jill, but it is to say "Goodby"; the swinging is a way of leaving childhood, leaving the moment, sweeping toward the stars. The motion is not only up high but also down deep. The movement is internal as well as external; there is stasis inside the motion, the small, still place where all possibility resides. The playground is literal and figurative; the writer at work is the writer at play, rhyming, chiming, climbing.

In the section entitled "Learning to Live in the World," Stafford reestablishes the sweeping vision of some of his best early work. Two poems in this section deserve to be read closely. They contain what is best and most interesting of Stafford's techniques, but they also lead to a newer, less secure, way of looking at the world. It is fascinating to note the tentative quality of the content underneath the sure, even authoritative tone in which the poems present themselves. The first is called "The Little Girl by the Fence at School":

> Grass that was moving found all shades of brown,
> moved them along, flowed autumn away
> galloping southward where summer had gone.
>
> And that was the morning someone's heart stopped
> and all became still. A girl said, "Forever?"
> And the grass: "Yes. Forever." While the sky—
>
> The sky—the sky—the sky. (16-17, 55)

At first glance, this is the familiar poem from memory. But the poem does not examine the "life" of the girl, her effect on the speaker, any of the things that might be expected. Instead the poem focuses on grass going brown (dying) in the autumn, ushering the reader into the second stanza where someone's heart has stopped. *Someone* and *girl* are generic terms. This is not "Berky" or the real past recovered. This poem is about death—and how to understand it. The girl can't understand and asks, in a child's clear question, "Forever?" The answer is nearly instantaneous. The grass, which covers the graves, knows that it is "forever," but the sky (or rather, *while the sky*, suggesting an alternative) . . . Here the poem falters. There is no alternative; the sky has no other answer. The sky simply *is*. In fact, as it repeats itself four times, the sky, too, is forever. One is reminded that, for Stafford, north simply is, and God. The sky endures, repeats itself endlessly, offers only the hope contained in that knowledge.

The second poem in this section is a major poem, and one that presents problems of interpretation. Entitled "Ask Me," the poem is an extension of the questioning mode characteristic of Stafford. It builds on implied questions, on questions that the writer supplies to the reader so that he can then contemplate the answers. Its convoluted logical system is part of its fascination. Made up of two, nearly equal, seven-line stanzas with long, sweeping lines that turn corners, weaving themselves into sentences, which, in turn, weave into the fabric of the poem, this poem simulates the deep, swirling movement of a river:

> Some time when the river is ice ask me
> mistakes I have made. Ask me whether
> what I have done is my life. Others
> have come in their slow way into
> my thought, and some have tried to help
> or to hurt: ask me what difference
> their strongest love or hate has made.
>
> I will listen to what you say.
> You and I can turn and look
> at the silent river and wait. We know
> the current is there, hidden; and there
> are comings and goings from miles away
> that hold the stillness exactly before us.
> What the river says, that is what I say. (19, *56*)

The first two words indicate the tentative nature of this venture—"some time" in an inexact future. "Ask me whether / what I have done is my life." What else, one wonders, could a life be? And, of course, the Stafford insistence that life happens somewhere inside and is not "done" springs immediately to mind. The startling question of this stanza is "what difference / their strongest love or hate has made" with its shadowy implications that the answer might be "not much." The nature of life itself is thrown into question—its complicated braiding of internal and external, solitary and shared experience, success and failure.

The second stanza seems to be reverting to Stafford's standard vocabulary—"I will listen." But this time the listening is only a willingness to take another point of view into account, to contemplate a question, but not necessarily to be in tune with an answer, even a "poetic" one. The river, so long a symbol of flux and depth, is stilled. The current is there only on faith, because of what the speaker knows and accepts of the physical world. Whatever is happening underneath the surface (the "comings and goings from miles away") is held in the stillness. The frozen river embodies the concept of motion in stasis, or vice versa. The stillness is exact; the motion is hidden. This is the contradictory message of the river. And Stafford is willing to let it speak for him—an enigmatic *ars poetica*.

The reader of the poem is left with more questions than have been answered. Just what conclusion is to be drawn from this nebulous statement? The answer, one suspects, is no conclusion; instead, it is an acceptance, a willingness to let some things exist in all their mystery. The speaker cannot say whether love or hate has made a difference in his life, cannot know the alternative lives he might have led as opposed to the real one he did, and is unwilling to commit himself to a simple, or simplistic, answer. He is willing to trust the currents and depths, the imperceptible meanderings of thought and feeling that also have comprised his life. He lives Whitman's words: "Do I contradict myself? Very well, I contain contradictions."[2]

"Ask Me" is quintessential Stafford. The surety of tone and the ease with which the words curl in on themselves draw the reader quietly into its complex structure. This is a poem to be read slowly, to be savored. It needs to slow down almost to the point of freezing so that the experience of its reading approximates the experience of its "message." The reader wants to hold the stillness of this poem exactly before him, and to sense the hidden currents in himself as well as in the speaker of the poem. To the extent that "Ask Me" insists on including the reader in the process of asking, the poem is universal. It becomes a mirror facing a mirror facing a mirror until the reader recognizes that the depth of his response to the poem does not lie in understanding an answer, but in understanding himself.

Over time, Stafford came to recognize the uncanny power of this poem, incorporating it into almost all of his readings as a kind of "signature." When Vincent Wixon and Michael Markee began making documentary videotapes for the Contemporary American Poets Series, they used "Ask Me" to open—and close—their first video, "What The River Says."

Things That Happen Where There Aren't Any People

In addition to the eight major volumes of poetry published by Harper and Row, William Stafford's published work included several other collections of poetry. Many of those were in beautifully printed chapbooks (for example, *Brother Wind*, 1986), or distinguished small press editions (such as *Smoke's Way* and *Roving Across Fields*, 1983). Some of these collections were comprised of poems that were not included in the trade editions; some were poems selected to follow certain themes. The small press books represent a further side of Stafford's character: he was generous and democratic. Almost every newly established magazine contained a poem by William Stafford. He willingly helped emerging presses and journals by lending them the stature of his name. For this reason, it is extremely difficult to compile a complete bibliography of Stafford's published works.

Some of the small press collections demonstrate an interesting facet of Stafford's work. By taking poems written over a fairly long period of time, and by pulling them together through their thematic concerns, these books illustrate the unifying vision of Stafford's poems. The poems lend themselves to re-ordering, to finding themselves in the company of other (earlier or later) poems. The fabric of his work might be seen as a plaid, with each theme represented by a separate color. In these books, the horizontal and the vertical of a particular color meet, forming that one tiny square of clear color. These limited editions and chapbooks reveal, in a variety of ways, the extent to which Stafford's work is all "of a piece."

For example, a 1978 pamphlet entitled *All About Light* contains eleven poems which highlight the difference, for Stafford, between the dark and the light. The poems concern light, matches, twilight, streetlights, sun, moon, stars, glass—sources of light—and also the internal light that comes with knowledge and understanding, the "bone light." Darkness is not seen as the negative of light, but as a positive force in which knowledge and understanding can grow. Darkness is not impenetrable, but invigoratingly accessible. Caves and dark rooms abound. But the dark allows for another kind of knowledge—for example, the fear of the hunted animal, or the hidden lives painted on the walls of caves. By concentrating on this motif in Stafford's work, this pamphlet calls attention to an attitude that allows contradictory forces their proper place in a larger order.

In 1986 Graywolf Press printed *Smoke's Way,* which performed a different function. This book collected out-of-print poems from Stafford's limited edition publications. These were organized in chronological order, and it became clear that almost any ordering of Stafford's work would reveal new shapes and facets. The gathering thread of this particular volume was the title poem which allowed for almost anything. Smoke's way is a "good way;" smoke diffuses, is there and not there, expands to fit the space, is "reluctant / but sure."[3] This, the poem implies, is the way of thought—and of poetry—and it will be "good."

In 1980 BOA Editions printed a collection entitled *Things That Happen Where There Aren't Any People*—poems that focus on the natural world or the solitary experience of it, poems in which such phrases as "every person gone" or "if no people come" or "sound nobody heard" are prevalent. Again, one is reminded of Stafford's "dream vision," the moment of transcendence that takes place in solitude. In the moral landscape of these poems things still happen; the world goes on, even if no one sees. In fact, as in "Answerers," the solitary nature of the exchange makes it possible for an internal alteration to take place:

> There are songs too wide for sound. There are quiet
> places where something stopped a long time
> ago and the days began to open

their mouths toward nothing but the sky. We live
in place of the many who stir only
if we listen, only because the living
live and call out. I am ready
as all of us are who wake at night:
we become rooms for whatever almost
is. It speaks in us, trying. And even if
only by a note like this, we answer.[4]

There is a sense here that the poem looks both forward and backward, by listening to the voices of people who have lived before and, at the same time, recognizing that the answer extends into the future, after the speaker too is gone. The "note" is the poem, trying to speak the ineffable, the song "too wide" (or too far?) for sound.

Death is a character in this collection. "Nobody" suggests a figure that is preceding the poet across the snow; the writer must walk faster and faster in order to fill the tracks. It ends with the image of a merging—writer with figure—and "you will no longer need to make those tracks in the snow" (10). The business of living will be complete and there will be a harmony in death. The distance between what is human and the forces of nature will narrow until no differentiation can be made.

Things do happen where there aren't any people: sunlight still finds leaves; water flows; the uninhabited world has meaning. For people, though, meaning comes through an understanding and acceptance. The final poem, "An Offering," accepts the presence of death in life, but uses the familar vocabulary that, by now, alerts the reader to the equation: shadow equals darkness equals imagination equals fusion with an ongoing legend equals death. Light, here, "when day stares too hard," is a burden from which we need to be saved. The first stanza poses a question:

Had you noticed—a shadow
that saves us when day stares
too hard?—inside our eyes
there's this shadow?

The poem hovers on the verge of knowing something "you almost know." It suggests that failure has its positive effects, and it ends by answering its own question and by giving its "offering:"

> And there is one shadow so great
> we live inside it our whole life long.
> And it is here right now.
> These poems are for that shadow (38).

In an interview in 1988, Stafford talked about this particular poem:

> Let me say something direct outside of poetry, outside of that careful little dance attitude you have to take in a poem, flat-footedly. I feel that in this poem there comes that extra, outside, unknowable (and yet sustaining us) mysteriousness that surrounds, and that instead of feeling put upon by that, lost by that, I feel comforted. I feel within myself a most definite alienation from those who feel that they have themselves encompassed the shadow, or this impossible-to-know, the presence of that. Instead of being frightening to me, I've come to count on it.[5]

The shadow, then, is seen to mean more than simply darkness or death. It signifies for Stafford an area of ineffable mystery—a place to test the limits of human knowledge.

This collection, with its narrower focus, allows readers to experience death as a major theme, where previously it had been a nebulous undercurrent in Stafford's poetry. "These poems are for that shadow." Mortality is the shadow within which everyone lives. The offering is poetry itself—not as a stay against death, but as a natural celebration of living. In collecting these particular poems and placing them in this order, the book emphasized the "things that happen" in the wilderness. The poet's confrontation with the personal specter of death marked a new direction in Stafford's work.

6

Any Sight, Any Sound
A Glass Face in the Rain and *An Oregon Message*

A Glass Face in the Rain

The "shadow" that Stafford recognized in *Things That Happen Where There Aren't Any People* was slightly different from the shadow that haunted the earlier books. Because it was so impersonal, it had to be internalized. In the process Stafford seems to have faced the shadow of his own death. In so doing, he found new areas for exploration.

Each section of *A Glass Face in the Rain* begins with a poem about writing. This type of poem is instantly recognizable, but what is new is the fact that they are displayed (each is set off in italics), and together they form a book within a book. They are self-conscious, and they make readers self-conscious as well. Do they have the capacity to read as Stafford expects them to? The dedicatory poem, "Smoke Signals," says "There are people on a parallel way."[1] It goes on to say that the book is for anyone, but "especially for those on that parallel way." It invites the readers in, and asks each of them to figure out whether he or she is one of those "parallel" people.

A Glass Face in the Rain comes back from the "edge"—that place where people don't quite figure—and roots itself in the real world again. Titles give us a hint of this: "A Touch on Your Sleeve," "Looking Across the River," "Passing a Pile of Stones," "Class Reunion," "Yellow Cars," "School Days," "With Neighbors One Afternoon." Stafford returns to his memories; perhaps the most poignant one is in "Remembering Brother Bob," where he recalls taking his little brother ice-skating and being insensitive to how cold he was. He threatened never to take him again, and, of course, realizes now—years later—that he never did. In poems such as these, one cannot refer to the speaker in the poem as the persona or the speaker without realizing how closely this speaker resembles Stafford the man. His brother, Bob, was five years younger. Stafford names him in the title, refuses to let him stand for an idea. His brother was a real person, and the regret at the way he had treated him is also real. The poems are part of the life, and a way of assessing the life.

"Glimpses" gives a sense of how the older Stafford is going to go on with that assessment. "One time when the wind blows it is years / from now." Time telescopes for him, containing the detailed memories from the past, and glimpses of a future. From this indefinite future the poem comes back to the present of the speaker, the presence of his mind:

> Walking along, any time,
> I find clues to tomorrow—how hard
> a poppy is orange, how alert the leaves
> are where the streetlight finds them.
> My debt to the world begins again,
> that I am part of this permanent dream. (21)

In the deep color of a flower, or the leaves suddenly seen fresh in the streetlight, the world comes clear again. The clues to tomorrow are in the lived life of today. The "permanent dream" (the world spinning through time, as in the earlier poem "Vocation") includes him again. The inclusion carries with it a responsibility, and *A Glass Face in the Rain* chronicles the dual nature of that responsibility. The poems about writing are self-conscious in that they carry an awareness that the writing is not merely representation of the world but a story of its own. On the other hand, the poems of the world contain the knowledge that they are distorted by time, sensibility, and the "dream."

One telling poem, though, calls itself "How To Get Back." The return from the dream is not easy, but Stafford's direct second-person address to the reader has the authority of a teacher or guide:.

> By believing, you can get there—that edge
> the light-years leave behind, where no one
> living today survives. (29)

The poem asserts that it is possible to come back, to let everything turn ordinary again. As "you" return, the people around will never be aware of the nature of "belief." The poem ends with, "They've never been gone." To make oneself one with the dream is the particular job of the poet/dreamer/believer/explorer. Everyone has the capacity, but not everyone will follow its call.

Poems about war creep into this peacetime book. This fact is due to more than the time between the writing of a poem and the production of a book. Stafford gives one of his central political concerns—war—free play at a moment when it is not the pressing national concern it once was; likewise, he represses it when it is in the news, as if he were afraid to sound too political or didactic. The Vietnam era was over, but unrest existed throughout the world. At any moment, it could explode. The poems warn us of that. "Not Very Loud" begins with the image of moths crowding around lights and beating at windows and doors. But this familiar sight soon turns in Stafford's slant vision:

> What are moths good for? Maybe they offer
> something we need, a fluttering
> near the edge of our sight, and they may carry
> whatever is needed for us to watch
> all through those long nights in our still,
> vacant houses, if there is another war. (25, *190*)

"Things I Learned Last Week" is also a warning, but the warning is slipped into a poem that is, for the most part, quite humorous:

> Ants, when they meet each other,
> usually pass on the right.
>
> Sometimes you can open a sticky
> door with your elbow.
>
> A man in Boston has dedicated himself
> to telling about injustice.
> For three thousand dollars he will
> come to your town and tell you about it.
>
> Schopenhauer was a pessimist but
> he played the flute.
>
> Yeats, Pound, and Eliot saw art as
> growing from other art. They studied that.

If I ever die, I'd like it to be
in the evening. That way, I'll have
all the dark to go with me, and no one
will see how I begin to hobble along.

In The Pentagon one person's job is to
take pins out of towns, hills, and fields,
and then save the pins for later. (66, *195*)

Under the guise of miscellaneous facts or observations, Stafford builds a poem that points out the ironies of this world. Art, for him, cannot be "studied" in order to create art. His death will take some practice; he'd like the cover of darkness. The reader might expect the poem to end with this personal revelation—what he has learned during the week—but instead the poem pushes on into what is prosaic and even flat. The person in The Pentagon taking pins out of towns is an ominous reminder that death is everywhere. The pins are saved for later. Everyone is "marked." Stafford may be able to joke about his own death, but the programmed death of others is no laughing matter, and is, finally, the focus of this poem.

"We Interrupt To Bring You" tells of a time in the future when the speaker misses the bomb. It's on the way; warnings have been given; but somehow he misses it. And then the people are dead; the television is blurry; but the world is there, and he has still missed the big event. These poems are effective precisely because the reader believes, as he reads, that these poems warn us of something real. Imagination is the force that gives us pause.

A Glass Face in the Rain does move into new territory, and that territory is an acceptance of the death of the individual. The "practice" deaths of the earlier books are now more fully imagined. There is a clear sense of self-effacement, a wiping clean of the slate. "A Glass Face in the Rain" imagines eventual disappearance as "you'll turn / aside at a fold in the earth and / be gone from the day" (57, *192*). In this poem, death is an absence of sight: the land will "stare blank for miles." It needs the human eye to come alive. Those who remember well will see a glass face, "invisible but still and real," in the rain. The rain, the window, the glass face—all blend to a clear, colorless ghost. Memory will persist, but the erasure of the body is complete.

Stafford imagines alternative deaths. "Yellow Flowers" does not have this simple disappearance. Instead, there is a wreck. It begins with "While I was dying." The imagination here takes the speaker right up to the "edge." He sees some yellow flowers on the side of the road and hears his pulse begging him to come back. Then he remembers a candle in church (triggered by the yellow flower). The end of the poem is an affirmation. Life is the religion. The world is the church.

> World with your flower, your candle:—
> we flicker and bend; we hear wheels
> on the road—any sight, any sound—that music
> the soul takes and makes its own. (103)

"Any sight, any sound." Stafford picks up his own metaphors, his own mythology, to bring himself back to the world of the living.

Stafford contemplates a future in which he will not exist. *A Glass Face in the Rain* is not a coming to terms, but it clearly toys with the idea of his own death. That seems to have made it possible to extend his imagination beyond the world and into the universe. Partly because of technology and partly because of this new frame of mind, some of the poems turn toward the effort to send messages into space, to communicate with other possible forms of life. The first poem in this volume, "Tuned In Late One Night," begins:

> Listen—this is a faint station
> left alive in the vast universe.
> I was left here to tell you a message. (15, *187*)

The word *message* becomes part of the heightened vocabulary that unlocks the poems. This is a departure from his previous books, and here he refers to poetry in this way; "message" implies speaker and spoken to; implies something to communicate, not just a simple acceptance of a train of thought. There is new urgency, a need for connection with the reader.

"A Message From Space" turns the words back on themselves. Workers have built an antenna to aim at the stars and are sending their Morse code out to the universe. Technology seems to offer positive as well as negative possibilities. But sometimes "we turn up / eye and ear" hoping to hear something back from out there.

The still voice that comes, however, says, "'Everything counts. The message is the world'" (61, *194*).

The final poem in the book is called "From Our Balloon Over The Provinces." It looks at the earth from above, and the particular angle of vision is telling. Stafford is removing himself, becoming the observer once more. The lesson of the earth is one of sound (the rooster) and sight (the roads and fields). The poem covers seasons, as though the balloon were floating for ages, fusing time. In the end, the indifference of the earth is noted:

> the world out there—not caring who
> we are—reaches us millions of ways:
> little fireflies quiet as truth
> climbing their invisible trellis of dark (117).

Fireflies climb the dark. Stars fill the sky. Truth comes quietly to the listener and observer. The message is there to be read.

An Oregon Message

Cheat Grass

If you are reading this, please
turn toward a window. Now think
of a field of cheat grass in a storm,
those little heads doddering and
shining their hint of purple,
but you can't tell why.

If you are still reading this
maybe something about that
grass comes back: it was
a trembling day with strange
noises. Whatever next thing
was coming, nobody knew.

No need to read any more—now
the cheat grass is still running
with the wind, rippling purple
waves. You could see it if

> you still lived there. And whatever
> the next thing was, it has already happened.[2]

"Cheat Grass" was printed in *Brother Wind*, a hand-set chapbook. Here Stafford demonstrates the flow of time from present to past to present, a present that now contains the past. He includes the reader in each stanza by insisting on the self-conscious act of reading. He then asks the reader to enter the realm of the imagination—to think of a field of cheat grass (a wild grass with rough blades and wheatlike ears). He uses the imaginative field to build a story that extends into the present, where the real fields of cheat grass are still "running with the wind." Time is set in motion and, at the same time, held still while the reader moves in and out of an imaginative *space*. Stafford insists on showing the reader how to enter that space by showing that he (the speaker) has also been there, can describe the grass and the impending storm, and the sense that something was about to happen. What happened, though, was back there, in the imagination, and now (in the present tense ending of the poem) it has already happened. Whatever it was, it can only be known in that imaginative space inhabited briefly by writer and reader alike. This inclusive attitude, with its accompanying rhetorical gestures, has been noted before, but it dominates Stafford's next book, *An Oregon Message* (1987).

In this volume the undercurrent has risen to the surface and he gives "message" the significance only hinted at in the previous book. The poems are preceded by "Some Notes on Writing," three short paragraphs which constitute an explanation of his writing method and methodology. This miniature essay is in a sense his first "message"; in no other volume has he felt it necessary to explain his poetry in a prose statement. Calling his poems "organically grown," Stafford defends his method against what must be seen as hidden critics. Why these words, and not some others? "Because these chosen ones must survive as they were made, by the reckless impulse of a fallible but susceptible person. I must be willingly fallible in order to deserve a place in the realm where miracles happen."[3]

Since this statement did not sound substantially different from his other available prose statements, the reader might wonder why Stafford felt compelled to state this at such a late stage in his career.

The answer may lie in the new way this book included the reader, almost from the first poem, as part of its subject matter. Therefore it asked the reader to be fallible with him.

The first section is called "The Book About You," and many of the individual poems, while speaking of the poet's life, suggest that his life and the reader's coincide. "You" and "I" are almost equated. Many of the poems speak directly to a listener, as though the reader were there in the room having a conversation with the poet. "The Big House" weaves the phrase "you know" throughout the poem, both to establish a colloquial tone and to insist on the participation of the reader. "A Voice From The Past" begins with inclusion: "I never intended this face, believe me" (19). The reader is drawn into the argument. Multiple tenses merge to create a link between the poet's personal reflective time and the reader's present; a new "present tense" is established on the page. By using small, indicative gestures, Stafford often ensures that the present tense of the poem will occur *only* in its reading:

> You who come years from now to this brief spell
> of nothing that was mine: the open, slow passing
> of time was a gift going by. I have put my hand out
> on the mane of the wind, like this, to give it to you.
>   (17)

"Like this." The reader is expected to *see* the hand reach out and to *feel* the way it includes him in the action. "Let's assume," begins one poem; "Forget the rain," begins another; still another addresses the readers, "O citizens." There is even a fill-in-the-blank poem ("Final Exam: American Renaissance") with slots for the answers. The reader of this book is expected to inhabit it, to become one of its characters. In this sense the "story" we are all "in" is the subject of the book.

At the same time that this all-inclusive stance is being perfected, *An Oregon Message* also reverts to a former pattern. There are more poems from the past (real places, real people) than in any volume since *Traveling Through the Dark*. There is a feeling of assessment. The opposing strains of father and mother are pulled together; they still are seen as polarities (even their way of dying is contrasted: the mother with fear to express, father who "quietly left"), but the speaker seems to be working toward some fusion. The father's "way," for so long the focus of Stafford's work, is now balanced by several poems about his mother. "A Memorial For My Mother" admits the divergence of their lives, and recognizes that some part of her is contained within him.

> Mother, you and I—

> We knew if they knew our hearts they would blame.
> We knew we deserved nothing. (105, *227*)

A recognition of his mother's voice in his was stated much earlier in an interview with Cynthia Lofsness:

> . . . and it's also just a statement of what I feel to be the truth, that when I notice little turns of speech, and attitudes toward events and people, I sense the presence of my mother's nature and her way of talking and a certain kind of not very assertive, but nevertheless, tenaciously, non-committal judgmental element that was in her. Not to assert very much, but on the other hand, to assert what she felt."[4]

Certainly one of the most striking poems in this book is "1940." Harking back to "Traveling Through the Dark," taking some of its key images and its formal structure from that work, this poem is equally elegant in its restraint. Four three-line stanzas with a scattering of slant rhymes, internal rhymes, and sound "chimes," this poem moves simply and inevitably down the page, much as the speaker is about to move on into his life:

> It is August. Your father is walking you
> to the train for camp and then the War
> and on out of his life, but you don't know.

> Little lights along the path glow under their hoods
> and your shoes go brown, brown in the brightness
> till the next interval, when they disappear in the
>   shadow.

> You know they are down there, by the crunch of
> stone
> and a rustle when they touch a fern. Somewhere
> above,
> cicadas arch their gauze of sound all over town.
>
> Shivers of summer wind follow across the park
> and then turn back. You walk on toward
> September, the depot, the dark, the light, the dark.
> (96, *225*)

It is important to note that the speaker includes the one who is spoken to by using the second person singular, "you." Stafford insists on making this a universal poem. It is *your* father walking *you*. This is the last moment of dependence. Again, the poem is about ignorance—or innocence—and the knowledge that can be gained only after traveling through the dark. Here sight acknowledges the shoes (as seen in the streetlight) and sound takes them on faith (as heard in the crunch of stone and rustle of fern). "Cicadas arch their gauze of sound all over town"; the poem includes everyone in its sheer canopy. The traveling takes the speaker into a new season—from summer to autumn and toward his own eventual death—and the reader perceives that the alternating intervals of darkness and light will make up the pattern of living from now on.

The use of the second person allows "1940" to make interesting observations. The poem is intimate in its knowledge of detail, as though spoken to one (remembered) person (the self?). The poem moves through time and space. The first short sentence introduces the month, and evokes associations with the end of the season. Next the speaker recognizes that this specific moment will connect to the future: "and then the War / and on out of his life." The omniscient voice of the poet intrudes for just one phrase: "but you don't know." The only thing one can be certain of is uncertainty. Is this a moment of hindsight? Humanity's continual state as it hovers on the verge of the future? The writer's trigger for imagination? Stafford allows for each of these—and more. The phrase describes the human condition. Causing a shiver similar to the "summer wind," it carries all the weight of premonition.

The "gauze of sound" in this poem is worth noting. The slant rhymes in "you," "know," "shadow," "town" help the lines turn on themselves; the internal weaving of sound (such as in glow/go, brown,brown/down, stone/fern, crunch/rustle/touch/above, over/shiver, park/back/ walk/dark/dark casts its own gauze over the poem; the use of the consonant *r* serves as a reminder that something hard is taking place here, the "crunch" of stone signals one life left for another. There is no end to the intervals until the final darkness.

Although "1940" would seem to be yet another poem looking · toward death, it carries with it the particulars of memory that root it in a real year, a real place. *An Oregon Message* on the whole is rooted in the land in much the way the earlier books were. "Wovoka in Nevada" takes one more hard look at what the white race has done to the Indian's dream. No buffalo running in the wind. Now "you can walk on his dream and scatter / bottle caps kicked in the ditch" (131). Fast cars. The glitter and glitz of casinos. But if you listen at the railroad crossing you will hear the "reminder" —"Wovoka, Wovoka, Wovoka." The name is part of the land as it "legends" itself. The dream persists beyond the "blind" windshields that do not allow for insight, or hindsight.

An Oregon Message flagrantly blends the humorous, the nostalgic, and the prophetic. Stafford enjoys himself in "Thinking About Being Called Simple by a Critic," where he alludes to William Carlos Williams by opening: "I wanted the plums, but I waited." Then, sitting in the dark, he wryly finds solace in such a "friend," seeing his own life as so simple that there was no way to qualify his thoughts with "irony or anything like that" (29, *213*). "Serving with Gideon" is more serious, remembering his early stand against racism—and the attendant temptation to remain "one of the boys." But the act remains small compared to the sky, the stars, the vast cycle of human history. Because of its larger themes and its social conscience, "Serving with Gideon" might well be called the companion piece to "Thinking for Berky," and Stafford's move "toward the elevator man" could be called one of the "millions of intricate moves" toward justice.

An Oregon Message strikes deep; it is Stafford's most consistent book since *The Rescued Year*. The poems are inhabited by people and the shape of human life. The speaker is openly engaging as he draws the reader into his remembered world. In addition, Stafford's sight on the world is more direct in this volume, and the result is a series of sayings that reflect both his accumulated wisdom and his sense of irony:

> Truth, brittle and faint, burns easily,
> its fire as hot as the fire lies make—(26, *212*)

> The eye that can stand the sun can't
>   see in shadow. (84, *223*)

> In the backcountry a random raindrop
>   has broken a dam. (135)

These little "messages" indicate the need to tell as well as to show. A didacticism creeps in. All the years of writing and being receptive have brought to Stafford some wisdom to be imparted—a sense of what it is to be alive and what is necessary for survival, a survival that requires being as tenacious as "The Bush from Mongolia," whose roots will not relax. "Some of us have to be ready," says the poem/poet/ speaker (140). Some of us must remember the past— and hang on. For Stafford, part of that survival is the daily practice of writing, like the daily run. In a poem more descriptive than prescriptive, Stafford uses that metaphor in "Run Before Dawn":

> Most mornings I get away, slip out
> the door before light, set forth on the dim, gray
> road, letting my feet find a cadence
> that softly carries me on. Nobody
> is up—all alone my journey begins. (119, *229*)

The poem goes on to describe what he passes, what passes him, what dream he finds himself in. It ends in the solitary vision of the creation of the poem:

> These journeys are quiet. They mark my days with
>   adventure
> too precious for anyone else to share, little gems
> of darkness, the world going by, and my breath, and
>   the road.

For William Stafford the morning "run" over the blank page was a way of living, a way of looking at and into himself, of keeping him honest. He faced himself in mirror after mirror, learning to own his own face more. Perhaps this was because, after staring at his eventual death, he opted for continued life. One poem from *An Oregon Message* suggests this and accentuates that self-examination. "Lie Detector" states that, whatever we do, our true selves will be discovered:

> You said it beats like a fist, proclaiming
> the truth all the time, hidden but always
> there, an emblem of what we need,
> a picture of how we are, slinking
> in honesty, frank as our hands
> or face, acting the self, helplessly true. (126)

But the second stanza contains its own "truth"—the world, the intensity of the present time and place, the realm where "miracles" (or poems) take place, and the heart making its own optimistic sound:

> At night, no one else near, you walk
> past fields, or trees, wind beginning
> its quest, a few stars glittering,
> an owl at home in the dark alone
> with its name—and your heart marching along
> with you, saying, "Now," saying, "Yes," saying,
>   "Here."

7

World Please Note
Passwords, Other Collections,
The Methow River Poems, *The Way It Is*

Passwords

Passwords, Stafford's ninth major collection, reveals a growing tension between opposing impulses toward the public and the private. The book opens with a series of "public" poems, many of them reflections on general themes, most of them told as "stories" the poet has heard. One early poem, however, is a personal story. "Reading with Little Sister: A Recollection" demonstrates how the act of reading makes the reader enter the story. The poem unfolds as though the story were theirs:

> The stars have died overhead in their great cold.
> Beneath us the sled whispers along. Back there
> our mother is gone. They tell us, "If you hold on
> the dogs will take you home." And they tell us never
> to cry. We'll die too, they say, if we
> are ever afraid. All night we hold on.
> The stars go down. We are never afraid.[1]

Stafford's revisions of this poem are recorded in the videotape, "The Life of the Poem," filmed by Michael Markee and Vincent Wixon. On the tape, its changing form is recorded, showing a gradual realignment of the basic sentences. The result is a kind of geographical location within the poem—overhead, beneath, back there—until the reader is centered on the sled, in the middle of the poem's emotional geography. Once again, the familiar "chimes" of sound carry the motion of the poem from "overhead/sled" through "cry/die" to "gone/on/down." And again, the ending is enigmatic, flies in the face of readerly experience by boasting that "we are never afraid" (what Stafford termed a kind of "nervous vaunting"). The title, however, suggests that they may be learning courage not through braggadocio, but through the imaginative act of reading.

"The Day Millicent Found the World" follows a girl into the forest until she becomes lost: "She had achieved a mysterious world / where any direction would yield only surprise" (9, 233). This is the state of the poet as he enters the poem, and to learn to lose yourself in the larger world is the ultimate goal. "That time she returned," but the poem hints that there will be a time when she simply becomes a part of the unknown.

The final poem of the first section, "An Archival Print," asks the reader to imagine that God "snaps your picture." As Stafford cautions the reader—"don't look away"—his observation becomes intensely personal: he's speaking outward, but he's making a private discovery at the same time. Stafford exposes the "self" here as a "partial disguise you call your character" (20, 236). There are influences and reasons behind what we are, he suggests, but

> The camera, wide open
> stands ready; the exposure is thirty-five years
> or so—after that you have become
> whatever the veneer is, all the way through.

The second section contains an important new poem. "The Summer We Didn't Die" speaks of a collective experience ("we played out there in the cottonwood") but is, perhaps, the most private of poems. Remembering a specific time in his past—"that year, that summer, that vacation"—Stafford recreates the emotions of the children climbing out on fragile limbs above adults who call them back in fear. A variation of a villanelle, "The Summer We Didn't Die," ends with the repeated phrase: "We were young. We had to be brave" (30). The title, however, adds hindsight; reader and poet alike face the dangerous implication that bravery is not always sufficient.

Throughout the book, a complex of words and phrases reveals a new thematic element for Stafford. "Scarier," "afraid," "never afraid," "scared," "brave," "fears," "shivers," "afraid even now"—the words occur in that order, leading inevitably to one of the later poems and the phrase "if you survive." This hints at a temporal urgency in *Passwords*; its "moment" (or time sense) contains an instance of personal loss and the various fears that surround such a loss. If Stafford seemed to come to terms with death in his two previous books (*A Glass Face in the Rain* and *An Oregon Message*), *Passwords* demonstrates otherwise. Stafford's oldest son, Bret, had recently died. The fourth section, entitled "Elegies," explores private grief by attempting to give it a larger and more universal context. "For a Lost Child" tries to fuse loss with the abstraction of time, but fails: "You are a memory / too strong to leave this world that slips away / even as its precious time goes on" (60, 244).

The section's title is in the plural—and Stafford mourns many other losses, along with that of his son. The sequence mirrors the process of grieving; just when the poems seem to have found a resolution, Stafford undermines them with doubt or fresh pain. Such titles as "Going On, " "Consolations," "Security," "Rescue," and "Yes" imply a way to deal with loss. Many of the poems end with phrases such as "go on" or "let go", but often the poems do not let go, rather, they fly in the face of their titles, piling doubt upon doubt. "Going On" looks hard at the evidence of his son's death: "Then, the stillest / way a hand can be and still be, / it lies there in mine" (61). The final stanza seems, on the surface, to have found a degree of acceptance:

> Easy world, you gave it once—
> please quietly welcome it back,
> that hand.

But the word "easy" betrays an underlying skepticism. There is nothing easy about the world or death as Stafford represents them. Both require a kind of inward attentiveness. A sense of mortality drives the poet to examine the self as when "Your Life" takes a long look (in the second person) at the idea of death where you will be "more real, more true, at the last" (70, 247). Stafford says, "You learn what you are, but slowly," and then, in a line that certainly includes himself, he discovers "a self often shattered"— a self that is essentially effaced in the glass, become no more than its past.

Stafford may have failed to conquer fear or accept death, but *Passwords* culminates with a powerful final section, "Vita." Here, in thirteen pieces clearly dominated by the first-person singular, he retraces his life, touching on old themes and finding once more the source of his poetry—and possibly his "self." "What's in my Journal" is especially telling for it lists several things that matter to him but also includes such items as "clues that lead nowhere" and "deliberate obfuscation, the kind / that takes genius" (75, 248).

Central to this section is a significant poem. "Life Work" is reminiscent of Stafford's most famous poem, "Traveling Through the Dark," but whereas in the earlier poem the speaker had to confront the harsh reality of animal life and death before traveling on, in "Life Work" he is more closely identified with the physical self and, by extension, with death. As in his earlier poem, Stafford calls up a specific time and place:

> Even now in my hands the feel of the shovel comes
>   back,
> the shock of gravel or sand. Sun-scorch on my
>   shoulders
> bears down. The boss is walking around barking.
> All the cement mixers rattle and jolt.
>
> That day the trench we are digging goes deeper
> and deeper, over my head; then the earth heaves
> in one giant coffin gulp. They keep
> digging and pulling and haul me out still breathing.
>
> The sky, right there, was a precious cobalt dome
> so near it pressed on my face. Beside me my hands
> lay twitching and begging at the end of my arms.
> Nothing is far anymore, after that trench, the
>   stones. . . .
>
> Oh near, and blessing again and again: my breath.
> And the sky, and steady against my back, the earth.
>   (80, 250)

The recounted accident allows him to experience his body in a new relationship to earth and sky: "Nothing is far anymore." This is not the willed mobility of "Traveling Through the Dark," where the speaker goes on with his life in the face of nature, but a stasis, an almost mystical acceptance of the interrelationship of life and death. In the final couplet, this acceptance is seen as a blessing which contains a kind of rehearsal for death. But the poem is called

"Life Work." He has been revived, brought up from within the ground to lie flat on it—and earth's the right place for love, though he'd never go so far as to say that.

"Life Work" is more formal than many of Stafford's poems, looking, on the page, more like one by Frost. Fourteen lines here almost equals a sonnet. And the alternating slant rhymes (back/barking, shoulders/jolt, deeper/keep, heaves/breathing, etc.) both cement the form and disrupt its expectations. The closest rhymes are found in the couplet (breath/earth), fusing the two so that they are virtually inseparable.

If there is one word that dominates this collection, it is "breath." Everything breathes—breezes, early morning, mountains. Words or thoughts go "on your breath out into the dark." Even the land was "invented by breath." Finally, death itself is imagined as a universal "breath" saying the names of his children. But breathing is both physical and individualized. Thus "The Size of a Fist" links survival to the heartbeat that pumps steadily through the lines, taking the man from infancy through schoolyard fights to work and family—and finally to old age ("who is this old guy?"): "beat, beat, engine cruising, day, night, / beat and away" (86, 252).

For all his public invitation, Stafford has remained intensely private. Though his poems embrace the reader, what greets us is not so much the man as the reflection he wants us to see. Reconciled briefly, the public and private coexist in the final poem "Vita." Stafford makes a distinction between *the* life and *a* life:

> God guided my hand
> and it wrote,
> "Forget my name."
>
> World, please note—
> a life went by, just
> a life, no claims,
>
> A stutter in the millions
> of stars that pass,
> a voice that lulled—
>
> A glance
> and a world
> and a hand. (88, *252*)

But where can the world take note, if not in the poems themselves? With supreme economy, the final stanza moves from individual vision outward and then back again to Stafford's recognizably symbolic gesture.

If his essential disguise (the one his character has hardened into) had been the "universal" self of the earlier poems, perhaps this book's new tension came from a burgeoning need to assert (and share?) the private self. Each of Stafford's books brought with it subtle shifts in perspective; now *Passwords* threatened to crack the "veneer" of the created self and release an even more powerful voice.

Other Collections, The Methow River Poems

In 1992, Confluence Press collected the poems from five previous chapbooks and published them under the title *My Name Is William Tell*, which subsequently won the 1992 Western States Book Award in Poetry. In citing Stafford's work, the judges stated:

> His way of writing and of offering his work stands in silent rebuke to all that is loud, strident, assertive and shallow. Yet close readers of Stafford's poetry know that there is a wildness at its center, by turns as gentle or tough as an undomesticated animal in an indifferent wilderness. He of course, presents his poems and himself as if they should be taken for granted. We would like to say on this occasion that we do not.[2]

This statement may be, in some measure, a response to Stafford's own somewhat defensive prose statement at the beginning of the book. Clearly smarting at some remarks that had classified him as a "regional" poet, he begins: "Being tagged a regional artist doesn't hurt much" (xiii). He goes on to say that art itself is regional, that it takes a kind of "sniffing along," that the artist can't look up to find a critic's approval or to discern the public's taste. The trail is "one-person wide." The artist is individual.

In a paper delivered at the Flint Hills Literary Festival in 1997, Stan Sanvel Rubin noted the "hurdles" of the front matter in Stafford's later books. In place of Stafford's usual gestures of greeting, Rubin found what he termed a "strategy of exclusion."

Looking at "You, Reader," the final poem in the book (the last full-length book to be published while Stafford was alive), Rubin notes the challenging tone—"the land rolls out its own / magnificence, and you inherit whatever your eyes / can prove by their glance that they're worthy of" (74)—and its concomitant question:

> Stafford was a habitual walker, but considering his method of composition in a state of physical stasis, the dynamic picture here raises a further question: is the reader in fact meant to be a companion—*sharing* the poet's journey by retracing the metaphoric "route" he already has taken towards inspiration—or is the poet metaphorically sending the reader away, abolishing the reader, so that he will remain in possession of (and possessed by) his own "world"?[3]

He goes on to compare Stafford's final stanza with Whitman's gesture of leave-taking at the end of "Song of Myself." Where Whitman says, "I stop some where waiting for you," Stafford commands, "Now, go back and begin again." The figure of the poet is decidedly different in each case. Stafford seems to have reversed not only the place of the poet, but the place of the reader. Whether this is a dismissive gesture or one that hands the reader more responsibility could be debated.

In 1996, three years after Stafford's death, a similar collection, *Even in Quiet Places*, was published by Confluence Press. This book also collects poems previously published only in chapbooks and has an extensive afterword by the poet's son Kim. It, too, contains an opening prose statement by the poet, but this statement, entitled "Another Language,"[4] is less defensive than in the previous collection. Defining the new language as one that "courteously gives credit to the needs but also to the dignity of the person addressed," as a language that refuses to distort or become self-serving, Stafford makes a quiet declaration of independence for "freedom in speech."

The opening poem, "Deep Light," reiterates the veiled challenge of the final poem in *My Name is William Tell* by suggesting that there are some people who, if they are not unworthy, are at least unaware, and therefore may not be able to enter the "far place" of the poem. The faint light hovering out there in the "deep night" is all the imaginative person will need:

From far a light, maybe a hill ranch
remote and unvisited, beams on the horizon
when we pass; then it is gone.
For the rest of our lives that far place
waits; it's an increment, one more
· hollow that slips by out there, almost
a gift, an acquaintance taken away.

Still, beyond all ranches the deep
night waits, breathing when we breathe,
always ready to offer new light,
over and over, so long as we search
for something so faint most people
won't know, even when it is found. (4)

Here Stafford deliberately equates the "dark" with the "deep."
The pronoun is plural—*we*; the poem speaks *for* as well as *to* us.
There is a kind of linguistic transformation; the night of the poem
becomes the light of the title. The darkness remains wholly outside,
yet it breathes when we breathe. It contains new light, available to
those capable of recognizing it, those who can participate in the
dream. By now, the farm light has become another recurring image,
but here it takes on the added dimension of something new.

The attitude in "Deep Light" is perhaps more skeptical than is
usually associated with Stafford. Darker, less hopeful than Frost's
great poem, "Directive," "Deep Light" echoes its speculative
emphasis on a lost place, a chosen recipient who must by definition
be "lost enough to find yourself."[5] Frost's quest for an attainable
grail becomes, for Stafford, a continuous search. In Frost, the cup
is hidden so the "wrong ones" won't find it. In Stafford's view,
they probably wouldn't recognize it if they did. Stafford does not
offer Frost's optimistic possibility of drinking and becoming whole
"beyond confusion"—he simply asserts that these faint lights do
exist, deep and ineffable, one more "far place" within the breathing
night.

Even in Quiet Places also contains a few poems that allude—
somewhat obliquely—to the Gulf War. Stafford's pacifism is
inherent in the poems—"Play like you had a war. Hardly anyone
/ got killed except thousands of the enemy" ("Pretend You Live
in a Room," 42) and "Back of history, leading afar / when the

armies marched / on the heads of the people, / was there a way too fine / for the blundering stumbling multitude?" ("Browser," 85)—but he refuses to make the specific war the point of the poem; instead he reminds the reader that overhead the stars keep telling their stories, that this is only one small piece of history in a longer history of violence that is "loose again."

The book culminates with a sequence of nineteen poems, called The Methow River Poems, written over a fairly brief period of time at the request of two forest rangers who wanted poetry road signs to place along a hundred-mile stretch along the Methow River. Six of these poems, along with "Ask Me," have since been etched and mounted along the roadway. The only truly distinguished poem in this series is "Ask Me" which had, by that time, become recognized as one of Stafford's most important poems. The rest have a conversational tone, seem less formal and more relaxed than most of his other poems, either digress or else end abruptly. In the "Afterword," Kim Stafford describes them:

> Some poems seem quickly made, hit or miss, almost random things, but with deft nuggets of insight. I think of Edward Weston's last photograph, that image of scattered rocks and sand at Point Lobos, a kind of reduction of universal spin to the elements of its original making. . . . I think also here of Joan Miro's late paintings from Majorca, the large, open canvases with a few bold strokes. (111)

The first of this sequence, "Being a Person," speaks directly to anyone who might stand by the river. "Be a person here," it urges. The idea of the shared dream is made explicit. If you listen hard enough, everything will converge: "Suddenly this dream you are having matches / everyone's dream, and the result is the world" (89). Stafford wants to embrace a unified country, a democratic place where all dreams converge to one dream. This desire is recapitulated in "Is This Feeling About the West Real?" where the speaker moves from a particularly regional outlook (where people know they live in a hemisphere beyond what Columbus discovered) to a more inclusive view of history. You can deny this world, the poem implies, but what happens outside—"whole mountain ranges, history, the holocaust, / sainthood, Crazy Horse"

(93, *176*)—demands your attention. There is an "other world" and the individual who can discover that place will have a vision to bring back to this one.

Perhaps the oddest of this sequence is "Emily, This Place, and You." The poem recounts how a woman named Emily got out of the car one day to watch the snow fill up the world. "It was quiet, you know" (101, *35*). The reader, too, can remember this place, "just being part of things, getting used to being a person, / taking it easy, you know." Often spoken informally to the reader, often referring to a specific place or sound or animal or tree in the immediate setting, the Methow River Poems focus on the world even as they seem to let it go. They hold the reader to the particulars of the landscape even as they demand the reader's attention with a series of informal instructions: "Nobody cares if you stop here"; "How you stand here is important"; "Please think about this as you go on"; "Hey, let's hurry down and forget this." At the same time, with all their enigmatic power, they proclaim a kind of poetic independence: "You see, there is something / beyond music"; "Stand here till all that / you were can wander away and come back slowly"; "What the river says, that is what I say." If these poems are regional, they are regional in its best sense; they speak of the place itself and of the interior space it generates. They embody every contradictory impulse Stafford ever felt—public and private, dark and light, physical and spiritual—and reconcile those impulses; the sound of the water becomes the sound of the poem. In this particular project, Stafford was able to realize a longstanding dream: "Instead of having all the effects of the poem be recognized while I'm there, I would like them just to linger after I'm gone, and no one needs to know what happened."[6]

The Way It Is

In 1998, Graywolf Press published Stafford's new and selected poems in a collection entitled *The Way It Is*—a title taken directly from one of Stafford's late poems, but echoing the ending of "Bi-Focal" where the world legends itself "deep, the way it is." The book itself is comprehensive, including all of Stafford's most significant poems and a number of representative poems from each stage of his career. The poems were selected by Kim Stafford, with help from the staff of the William Stafford archives as well as poets and critics across the country. The book opens with two sections of "new" poems—a selection entitled "Sometimes I Breathe" (written in 1992) from a book manuscript intended for publication, and one called "There's a Thread You Follow," written between January 1993 and his death in August.

These opening sections contain seventy-one poems and together they exhibit the same uneven quality seen in almost all of Stafford's books. Elegant and complex poems are accompanied by ones that feel slight in comparison; one might call this a lack of quality control, but this time it was not the poet himself who made the selections. This leads to the conclusion that Stafford's way of writing produced so many ideas, not all of which came to aesthetic fruition, that it is nearly impossible to create a tightly structured book. The strong poems that follow these sections further confirm this: they make a strong statement about the importance of Stafford's vision through careful selection of the best from over three thousand published poems.

There are few surprises in the new poems. They fit rather comfortably into the overall oeuvre—a combination of memories, observations, pithy statements, and tentative meanderings. Interestingly, many return to early themes. "Clash" revives the dormant duality of father and mother, unexpectedly rhyming the first and third lines of each four-line stanza, thus creating a "clash" of its own. The penultimate stanza steps back to take another look at the speaker's relationship with his mother:

> I won before too late,
> and—adult before she died—
> I had traveled from love to hate,
> and partway back again.[7]

The ending of the prose poem, "Something That Happens Right Now," reiterates the visionary concept of death found at the end of "The Farm on the Great Plains":

> Then my feet would come loose from Earth and rise by the power of longing. I wouldn't let the others know about this, but I would be everywhere, as I am right now, a thin tone like the wind, a sip of blue light—no source, no end, no horizon (8).

Nor had Stafford changed his attitude toward war, but the overtly antiwar poems are more strident, almost accusatory. "Right to Die" sets the tone: "God takes care of it for / everyone, once. And armies / figure it out, wholesale, / for others, in the air, on the ground, / at sea" (12). It is hard not to read the specificities of the Gulf War into some of the explicit contemporary allusions. "Entering History" ends with just such a note:

> Where was your money when the tanks
> grumbled past? Which bombs did you buy
> for the death rain that fell? Which year's
> taxes put that fire to the town
> where the screaming began? (10)

One noticeable change, however, is the open naming of Bret, Stafford's oldest son who had committed suicide. In *Passwords*, Stafford had relegated poems about his death to the category of "elegy" and had softened any specific references to generality. With the distance of time, he was able to come closer to the event. Written in 1992, "Third Street" looks back to a time when the poet had been ill as a child, thinking he might die. He remembers his father's look. Time is conflated as he concludes: "Years later my son will die and that look / will return. Something will break in the sky that was welded / and forged back home by a thousand pledges of truth" (5). His steady world was shaken. "A Memorial: Son Bret" begins "In the way you went you were important" (16) and then reveals regret over what they would not experience together. Still, the poem ends with a question—"remember?"—tying father and son to a time and a place they had shared. More disturbing is

"Crossing Our Campground" where the opening ("Part of the time when I move it's for / Bret") is tinged with an implied reproach:

> This is for you, Bret, I think; this
> is the way an old man walks who still
> stays vigorous and strong, firm, alert,
> holding on through the years for you—
>
> The kind of old man you could be,
>   or could have been. (*37*)

Although he had used his mother and father as symbolic dualities, with rare exceptions Stafford had not written so specifically about his immediate family. "Retirement" suggests that when the children have left, the rest of life is like driving into a snowstorm, "the soft / careful sound of little worlds falling" (28). For young readers who might not understand this sensation, the speaker states, "there will be time."

A large percentage of the new poems hark back to the beginnings—the farm on the great plains with its expanse of sky. These are the most fully realized of the late poems, often orchestrated in regular stanzas and emphasizing a web of sound. "Haycutters" invokes an almost idyllic (though not perfected) past. "One Evening" stills the remembered moment, almost like the "frozen pond a mile north of Liberal," where sixty years ago he skated "wild circles." The final stanza is urgent with longing:

> I would go home, confront all my years, the tangled
> events to come, and never know more than I did
> that evening waving my arms in the lemon-colored
>   light. (*11*)

"Living on the Plains" also resurrects a specific time and place—"If you come back years later your name / will be there carved on the windowsill / in the hayloft"—even as it also connects us to the American mythology—"If you ever climb the map again / you could stop there and whisper a few hymns, / the ones that civilized Dodge, Cody, Abilene" (41).

"Slow News from Our Place," catches up several of Stafford's abiding themes, creating an informal summation. Speaking directly to some of the influential American poets who had preceded him, he weighs their words in contrast to the permanence of the land:

> It isn't that the blossoms fall, Ezra.
> It isn't that certain vagueness, Wallace.
> It isn't even how those flies buzz,
> either, Emily. It's only the plains
> out here, how they take it all and wait,
> morning, evening, night, forever;
> how they don't move, no matter what
> Galileo says, or The Church, or God himself.
>
> We stand on the ground, out here. Go ahead,
>   speakers;
> tell us your theories, your judgments, the latest
>   assessments
> from the centers of power, any styles or truths you
>   like.
> We're out by The Platte, The Missouri,
> The Smoky Hill. We're quiet on this slow scanner
> The Earth, under its arch of sky.
> Go ahead. Tell us. We're listening. (34)

Inclusive (written in first person plural), but highly individualized in its particularities, the poem is strikingly full of doubt and defiance. Underneath its surface is a core of darkness. What does poetry mean in the vastness of forever? The answer, the poem suggests, is not to be found in theories, judgments, science, or religion, but in the active act of listening, of being receptive to whatever the world wants to tell us under its wide arch of sky. The late poems come full circle, back to their origins; to quote a line from Frost's "West-Running Brook," they are the "current paying tribute to the source."

8
Like a School of Fish
Stafford's Poetic Technique

Sound generates sound, rhythm suggests rhythms, and one image often pulls in a "coterie" of accompanying words to create the texture of Stafford's collective work. Specific words surface over and over, acquiring special meanings. Only through the weight of accumulated poems does the true significance of Stafford's vocabulary become clear. There is a consistency of usage that reveals basic thematic concerns and at the same time demonstrates his tendency toward the symbolic. It is necessary to pay attention to these repetitions. Some words seem to remain symbols for the thing itself, as, for example, *rain*. Others take on various degrees of symbolism. *Wind*, for instance, is often personified: wind "combs fields," "buries skulls," and becomes the "supreme caress." It is carrier of seed, of bird, of sound. Sometimes it becomes breath itself, a life force.

Most of Stafford's poems have at least one word that shimmers with difference. His verbs wander, are used in atypical, oblique ways: "until we pause / to flame what we know"[1] or "rescued by how the hills / happened to arrive where they are."[2] These constructions could not quite be called surrealism; they are evidence of a mind allowing for more possibilities within language than the ordinary dictionary would approve. Here is a writer experimenting, and—the lesson is clear—such receptivity to words will give new meaning to them. Although any given poem might show a usage that might seem imprecise, the cumulative effect is an "imprecision" that is more accurate than fact. Stafford manages to make certain words leap from the page simply by how he uses them. One example is *yeast* used as a verb. Stafford employs this construction ("yeasting," "yeasts along") often enough that a response is inevitable. The reader cannot deny his own associations with the word *yeast*—dough rising, constant change, warmth, fragrance, the promise of bread. Thus, if Stafford uses that word in connection with poetry, there is the promise of a poem.

It would be possible to select poems in which the use of a certain word would elucidate how that word functioned for Stafford. By watching one word, the careful reader is able to see how he used it in different circumstances, testing each shade of meaning. Constantly aware that his meanings were linked more to language than to object, Stafford demonstrated the Derridian slippages and linguistic play so valued by the critical approach known as deconstruction. Like Wallace Stevens before him, Stafford built a "language," or linking vocabulary, through which to enter his imaginative spaces. (Unlike Stevens, he used a seemingly transparent, even commonplace, vocabulary.) One way he did this was by playing on associative words. *Snow* often signals his poems about death ("The night my father died, the moon shone on the snow"[3]), but snowflake, blizzard, storm, ice, cold, shiver can substitute for the central image. Winter is the "snowy interior." Fear and cold are inseparable. And beyond winter lies the cold territory of the unknown and unknowable. *Beyond* and other words that denote distance are associated with this sense of cold otherness. Any of these words must be read with the larger, symbolic meaning in mind.

To make the reading even more complex, *snow* (especially a field of snow) is also associated with the blank page, and walking in snow is equated with writing. As the reader becomes more and more familiar with the way these words are used, he cannot deny the impulse to connect these two usages. To write is, in some sense, to die. The self disappears and the poem finds its own way. The white page and the snow-covered grave become (however briefly) identical.

The result is a vocabulary that hovers on the border of metaphysics, shading into implication by association. Read together, these poems come to seem mystical, but without mysticism. One must be careful not to reduce this vocabulary to a simple series of equations or to attempt to harness it into a system. To do so would create mis-readings. The reader must remain sensitive to the word in its context within the individual poem before he allows this extended vocabulary to influence his perceptions. *Dark*, for example, is often seen as the fertile ground for imagination. But *dark* also functions in the more traditional sense of ignorance and uncertainty, to say nothing of the literal night. Stafford's nephew, Patrick Kelly, in an appreciation in *Kansas Quarterly*, describes it as the darkness of nature, not the darkness of evil.[4] Stafford, when questioned, said, "I remember when I was a little kid, when someone would be afraid of the dark because you couldn't know what was there, I felt secure in the dark—maybe like a bat or an owl—because in the dark I knew as much as anybody else. And that's where we are—it's wonderfully soothing."[5] To "travel through the dark" is not the same as to be "led by my own dark." *Dark* and *light*, more than any of the other key words in Stafford's metaphorical vocabulary, vary in meaning and usage and must be examined carefully from poem to poem.

Thus, Stafford weaves a web of association; images refer to images, poems refer to poems, often calling up previous ones with repeated phrases or titles taken from the lines of other poems. A seam of vocabulary and reference connects the individual books to each other. Childhood games, as one example, weave themselves throughout the work—a warp of memory—to show how time can be conquered at will:

> With fingers crossed we cross
> their field, and hide, and call
> *Come find me! Oh, I'm here!*
> *I'm free! Not it! Not it!*
>
> They never move. No sound.
> And then the snow.[6]

> ✳✳✳

> And there is easy talk, for throwing
> back like Annie-Over, or a minuet,[7]

> ✳✳✳

> Till unbound by our past we sing
> wherever we go, ready or not,[8]

The hide-and-seek or Annie-Over of childhood provides a metaphorical way of looking at adult situations. The speaker contains the child he was, and that childhood is there for ready reference and association. Memory functions this way as well;

certain place names or people populate the poems (Kansas, Ella, as examples) to establish the full implications of a lost past. Time is abolished, the past is pulled headlong into the present tense. One poem that demonstrates the complexities of time in Stafford's work is "Strangers":

> Brown in the snow, a car with a heater
> in it searches country roads all yesterday afternoon
> for our farm. At crossroads the car stops
> and over the map the two people bend.
> They love how the roads go on, how the heater
> hums. They are so happy they can be
> lost forever that afternoon.
>
> They will probably live.
> They may die. The roads go on. On the
> checkered map they find themselves, and their
> car is enough audience, their eyes enough
> to know. If the state breaks off they will
> burrow at the edge, or fall. I thought of
> them yesterday, and last night sang by the
> fire, thinking of them.
>
> They are something of us, but I think better,
> lost back there in our old brown car.[9]

The first line contains the dualities of heat and cold; here the snow covers evidence of time. In the present tense, the car *searches*—all *yesterday* afternoon. This is grammatically impossible but emotionally possible, and Stafford is interested in the emotional truth. The voice is that of the knowing observer. As though watching a movie, the reader observes as the strangers, a couple, bend over the map. But the speaker of the poem has an inside knowledge, more than sight would allow; he can claim that they "are so happy they can be / lost forever that afternoon." The word *that* makes the afternoon specific—somewhere locked in time— and the yesterday represents the time of the memory, itself already buried in the past. To be "lost forever" on a specific afternoon might seem contradictory, but it accurately reveals the emotional state of the couple. They remain lost in this particular way because memory places them there in perpetuity.

The stanza break creates a break in the observer's stance. He speculates, almost as though he had not been perceived to have the inside knowledge felt in the first stanza. They may live or die. Only the roads are permanent. On the map they "find themselves"—not their place or location, but selves outside of geography. If the "state" breaks off (the "edge" again), their fate is unknown. But the speaker *thought* of them, *was thinking* of them. The tenses of the verb pull them, almost literally, into the present.

The final couplet completes this process: They are "something of us" (in the present), and the observer thinks better (present tense). The phrase is ambivalent—do they seem better than "us"? Or does he think better of his designation? The poem turns on its last line, spinning the speaker and the reader, "lost back there in *our* old brown car." The insider's vantage of the first stanza is reestablished; the speaker did have intimate knowledge of that couple. The second stanza was the speculation, the ongoing uncertainty as to what life will bring (as opposed to what it has already brought). They are literally "something of us"—the strangers hardly recognized in the photo album, the lost selves of the past who are found again, in memory.

Over and over again, Stafford defeats time and loss in this way. His poems move through time to make the past alive again, even as they contain a more dominant present tense. This layering of time is more truly accurate of the way people carry their pasts with them; language is the barrier, with its insistence that the past remain locked in its own tense. In this sense Stafford's depiction of time is Bergsonian. In Bergson's description, "Inner duration is the continuous life of a memory which prolongs the past into the present. . . Without that survival of the past in the present there would be no duration but only instantaneity."[10] Memory liberates the past, just as dream liberates the image. Perhaps, as Bergson has said, poets do "explain Time better than philosophers."[11] This may be because they are not so much analyzing the nature *of* time as trying to portray what it is to live *in* time.

For Stafford, narrative is often simply implied, something which moves behind the poems. The final synthesis comes not from the culmination of linear movement but from a fullness and complexity surrounding the lyric moment. The effect is not one of speed but of stillness—the moment held to the light. By holding still in this way, in a moment of intense awareness, he creates a form of consciousness. He sees himself in relation to the outside world. He unearths something close to archetype. Time hovers in these poems as one element of their form.

An alternative reading of "Strangers" might state that the "now" of the poem is "yesterday afternoon and evening" when the car is doing its searching and when the speaker was thinking of the couple. In this reading, the speaker is almost a visionary, creating the strangers who will inhabit a remembered space, looking for the farm. This reading places more emphasis on the speculations, which become the fiction writer's concerns: Will they live or die? What will their future be? But although this reading is possible, the dominant tense of the poem would favor the first reading because it allows for the specific memory which makes the "strangers" less strange. To divorce the poem from the personal is to reduce it to the realm of speculation, when otherwise it contains both nuance and true insight into the nature of memory. "Strangers" defeats time, but it does not deny it.

It is no coincidence that Stafford, whose poems exhibit this layered sense of time, was interested in philosophers and writers who address the issue. Reading Augustine's *Confessions*, he commented, "One of his speculations is about time—you know, beginnings and endings and forevers and what the past is if you look at it in the present. . . . I'm just tantalized and teased by it. I never have arrived, but I've had the fun of participating with someone as subtle as Augustine. In my poems, part of it is the abiding and delicious puzzlement about time."[12]

"Strangers" also demonstrates Stafford's sense of sound. The *o* of the first stanza weaves its various gradations of sound from line to line—brown/snow/roads/afternoon/our/over/ two/roads/go/so. This weaving extends to the shorter *o* of "love" and "lost." A similar effect is seen in the music of the internal *r*, which accentuates the *o* by seeming to move over and under it: car/heater/yester(day)/after(noon)/our/farm/car/over/heater/forever/after. The *h* makes itself obvious with a heavy alliteration in "how the roads go on, how the heater / hums. They are so happy," as though the word *happy* were a natural consequence of the heater and the humming. The *o* and *r* are wedded again in the last four words (linked by "better" and "back there")—"our old brown car." The surprise, here, is the word *old*, which roots the poem so firmly in the life and the memory. Stafford described his method of discerning sound in an essay called "Where 'Yellow Cars' Comes From":

> I like how the syllables do-si-do along. I am not after rhyme— so limited, so mechanical. No, I want all the syllables to be in there like a school of fish, flashing, relating to other syllables in other words (even words not in this poem, of course), fluently carrying the reader by subliminal felicities all the way to the limber last line.[13]

Stafford found rhyme mechanical because it imposes something on the external form of the poem when he wanted to see it grow organically. He was so receptive to the colloquial and the spoken language that his emphasis was on finding the poetic within an ordinary speech pattern. He found a way to create the effect of rhyme without its constrictions; his audible "school of fish," flashing through the poem, is most evident when the poem is read aloud. The sounds call attention to themselves and to their similarities with other sounds. In this way, each word is enhanced and made new again.

The near-rhyme, or slant rhyme—the sounds that unsettle the ear—might be termed Stafford's stock-in-trade. He used his keen ear to set up expectations that he then refused to meet. The result is an intensified participation in the reading of the poem as well as the pleasure of unexpected patterns.

Stafford used sound as a gauge to see if the poem had found its proper "trajectory in sound." This trajectory had to be recognized at the time, since it is not something the writer can plan:

> I think sound comes out of the language right while you're having the language. In myself, as a writer I feel at home with what's happening in the sound of the language I try to induce in myself right now. . . . Instead of thinking there is some kind of pattern you can achieve, I feel that there is this infinite appreciation possible for the way the language goes. It's not a station on the way to perfection; it's a kind of limber

accompaniment of what the language can offer in its
syllables, which have meaning themselves too subtle for us to
analyze, but always making an effect.[14]

Revision, for Stafford, was also a listening process. He waited
for the sound to "track right," looking for signals from the material
rather than from some predetermined set of meanings. "The
assessment of the product is something that happens *after* you've
done it. You should simply go ahead and *do* it. And do it, I might
add, without being critical."[15] "Revision—they say it as if it
suddenly has to turn mechanical, or has standards, but there isn't
any transition at which the creative process becomes the critical."[16]
Revision should be as natural as writing itself. If not, better to
abandon the attempt and go on with the long, sure process of
discovering the world. The meaning is in the doing.

Stafford also resisted the predetermined form of prosodic
structures. He used the stanza more as a unit of thought than as a
unit of measure, though he often carried his thoughts down the
page in a highly regular (three or four line) fashion. Both his early
and his later work exhibited a reliance on stanzaic units while the
"middle period" is characterized by a lack of precise stanzaic
structure. Rhythm, in the form of meter, is hard to detect, though
it is possible to make claims for individual lines of iambic
pentameter ("that world is with us and those wolves are here"[17]).
Usually the iambic beat is a ghost rhythm, a loom over which the
variations are constantly being shuttled, as in "On Main one night
when they sounded the chimes."[18] The poems may start or end
with a metrical pattern, but they rarely follow one from start to
finish. If Stafford has a characteristic line (and it is hard to discern
one), it hovers at around eleven or twelve syllables with three to
four strong beats or stresses ("where they can. And if any of us get
lost"[19]), and it often contains a caesura to stop it midstream. As he
shortens his lines, the beats become stronger ("I want that one."[20]).

There is, however, a characteristic *sentence* in Stafford's poems.
Phrase after phrase, the sentence builds around its commas; the
connections are sometimes vague, but Stafford relies on syntactical
construction to weld his images together. This technique also
allows him to change gear, modify ideas, qualify, or clarify, by use

of subordinate clauses. Many of his sentences begin with "if" or "because" and then move to the realm of conjecture. They vary in length, but the convolutions are almost a voice print. The contrast in the beginning of "Existences" is typical: "Half-wild, I hear a wolf, half-tame, I bark."[21] Even more sinuous is the final sentence of "The Earth"—a sentence that takes Stafford four and a half lines to complete:

> We come, we
> celebrate with our breath, we join on the curve
> of our street, never lost, the surge of the land
> all around us that always is ours,
> the beginning of the world and the end.[22]

The sentence becomes the unit while the line breaks add diversity. Stafford wrote little about line breaks but what he did say sheds some light on his method:

> Placement—the end of a line, for instance—makes a difference, but sometimes the difference is small; even if no pause, or little pause, occurs, the forward feeling of the poem will sustain a syncopation. . . .
>
> But to live your writing life by assuming that certain "norms" have been established and thereby made operative for any writer—such a stance reverses the actual: writers recognize opportunities. . .
>
> Any break at a line, any caesura, any surfacing of natural syllable intonation—these are all a total of language-feel that the writer orchestrates according to what comes along in the act of composing. . . .
>
> So, everything makes a difference: a word at the end or beginning of a line is different from a word elsewhere in the line.[23]

Stafford's lines do not break so much as spill down the page. Enjambment is the norm. Again, they can be described as deceptively simple. They thrust the poem forward at the same time that they contain a larger meaning in and by themselves. Just as the first line of "Strangers" contains the opposites of hot and cold, many of Stafford's lines (and breaks) work through surprise. "Traveling through the dark I found a deer / dead"[24]—the deer exists before it dies. Other lines wait for a qualification: "After that sound we weren't people / any more."[25] The break presents the reader with total annihilation before it goes on to clarify and explain. Or: "Some time when the river is ice ask me / mistakes I have made."[26] The poem hovers before the question is phrased, possibly before it is formulated. Others contain their own truth before they go on to a larger truth: "Little animals call / us."[27] They call whether we are there or not, but in this instance they are calling "us."

There is also a somewhat characteristic ending, which goes against the grain of expectation. While many of his poems reach for a new level of understanding and seem to find it (often in a last line set off from the rest of the poem), an equal number reflect a condition of partial knowledge. Closure, for Stafford, is not a way of summing up, or of reaching an epiphany. If anything, many of his endings undercut the emotional peak of the poems, falling off into prosaic conjecture and flat rhythms. Rather than reach for a false, poetic conclusion, Stafford remains true to the questioning nature of his poetry, with its attendant "failures."

Stafford's syntax is nowhere near as simple as his diction. He claimed to want to follow normal syntactical construction, but his deliberate variations create ambiguities that hold the reader's attention. "Farm girl away through the wheat"[28] is hardly a complete sentence, but the rest of the poem justifies this imagistic gesture. "Eyes that were still eyes"[29] uses the multiple meanings of "still" to layer the line with possibilities: are they persisting, fixed, hushed, deathlike? The ordering of the words is important; here, the syntax insists on multiple interpretations where a simple rearrangement would clarify, but limit, the meaning. "We know the motions of this great friend, / all resolved into one move, our stillness" makes no syntactical sense, but the reader gets used to deciphering such constructions and takes pleasure in sliding between contraries, in this case motion and stillness.

The poems reveal an awareness of the ambiguity and imperfection of language; this refutes critical views that his method, as well as his message, is "simple" or transparent. Indeed, considered in this light, his work may be as suitable for the kind of sophisticated linguistic analysis engaged in by contemporary literary critics as it has been for New Critical analysis. In other words, from the very beginning of his career, Stafford was avant-garde.

A combination of these effects creates the specific voice associated with a Stafford poem. Familiar images rise to the surface; lines spill and halt; sound unfolds, making its own sense. "Vespers," the final poem in *Someday, Maybe*, uses each of these characteristic techniques to weave its complex tapestry: the end of day, a sense of dying, of shedding the past. To this end, Stafford uses phrases ("ready or not") from childhood, such key words as *wind, rock, west, home, sing, prayer*. The progression of these words, ending on a religious note, is part of the way this poem means. Rhymes are more evident in the first stanza, giving way to sound associations and repetitions by the second, and a complex of internal ("prayer" and "are") and end rhymes ("end" and "friend") culminate the third. Some lines have their own integrity ("every fist the wind has"—it has a fist before it loses it). Others begin to spill over, creating urgency ("wing and / then wing over the valley / and over the valley, . . ."). Time is slowed, savored, then stopped ("stillness above and below"). The poet begins in the abstract, moves to the specific, then into the realm of memory and emotion, and finally speaks directly to someone—a someone embodied in the reader:

> As the living pass, they bow
> till they imitate stones.
> In the steep mountains then
> those millions remind us:
> > every fist the wind has
> > loses against those faces.
>
> And at the end of the day
> when every rock on the west
> claims a fragment of sun,
> a last bird comes, wing and
> > then wing over the valley
> > and over the valley and home,

Till unbound by our past we sing
wherever we go, ready or not,
stillness above and below, the slowed
evening carried in prayer toward the end.
  You know who you are:
  This is for you, my friend.[30]

9
Willingly Fallible
The Essays/The Art

When William Stafford retired from Lewis and Clark College in 1980, he had been teaching there for thirty-two years. Over those years he also led summer workshops at colleges and writers' conferences across the country, including such prestigious programs as The Breadloaf Writers' Conference. His essays on the teaching of writing have become well-known—and often criticized as making a difficult process sound altogether too easy, as being too accepting of a given piece without demanding rigorous standards. It is easy to see how these criticisms could arise, but not so easy to see why the critics have not understood what Stafford had to say. His theories of teaching came directly from his theories of writing, not the least of these what writing can, and should, do for the life of the writer. Given this specific context, his theories were consistent with his statements, not only on writing and revising, but on living as well.

In 1970 an essay by William Stafford appeared in one of the first issues of *Field*, a magazine produced at Oberlin College. Titled "A Way of Writing," the essay seemed to challenge the critical tenet of authorial intentionality by suggesting that the writer might not, after all, know exactly what he was doing. Or saying. He suggested that the writer might, instead, be trusting to something larger than himself, something he too must take on faith. Although this is no surprise to many writers, it certainly makes the discussion of poetry in the academic classroom much more equivocal. Stafford outlined his own process, emphasizing his spirit of receptivity:

> So, receptive, careless of failure, I spin out things on the page. And a wonderful freedom comes. If something occurs to me, it is all right to accept it. It has one justification: it occurs to me. No one else can guide me. I must follow my own weak, wandering, diffident impulses.

> A strange bonus happens. At times, without my insisting
> on it, my writings become coherent; the successive elements
> that occur to me are clearly related. They lead by themselves
> to new connections. Sometimes the language, even the
> syllables that happen along, may start a trend. Sometimes the
> materials alert me to something waiting in my mind, ready
> for sustained attention. At such times, I allow myself to be
> eloquent, or intentional, or for great swoops (Treacherous!
> Not to be trusted!) reasonable. But I do not insist on any of
> that; for I know that back of my activity there will be the
> coherence of my self, and that indulgence of my impulses will
> bring recurrent patterns and meanings again.[1]

In this statement it is possible to detect the specific rules that guided Stafford's writing. First, the resistance to rules, the willingness to see what will happen. Second, the reliance on self as the ultimate authority and the confidence that that self will be the shaping force underneath every poem. Third, a responsiveness to language itself—the syllables that "happen along"—and the possibility that "sound" may shape meaning at least as effectively as sense. Fourth, a suspicion of what is "reasonable," or the converse, that resisting reason may in fact produce a deeper, more profound, kind of reason. Fifth, a willingness to fail, which implies a critical sense, one that can recognize the relative success or failure of the poem to produce a coherence. But the process itself is what is important; the insights to be gained in following this prescription go far beyond the possible "successful" poem. The recurrent patterns tell him something about what is important to him, about the nature of his imagination, about the world of language that he inhabits.

Stafford in prose is still the Stafford of the poetry. It is interesting to note the vagueness of the language Stafford uses to describe this process—and the sureness of the tone. He is convinced of the rightness of his method (for himself), is certainly in tune with the process as he practices it, but cannot define with precision just what it is. Syllables "happen along." As a writer, he knows this. As a reader, he knows that critics talk as if this were not the case, as if every word were chosen for a particular purpose or end within the poem. In "Some Arguments Against Good Diction," he carefully talks about the differences between practicing the craft and *talking about* the practice of the craft. Constantly aware that language distorts even as it tries to make clear, Stafford is trying to clarify an attitude, not a method. "Where words come from, into consciousness, baffles me. Speaking or writing, the words bounce instantaneously into their context, and I am victimized by them, rather than controlling them. They do not wait for my selection; they volunteer."[2] He makes this statement more explicit in an essay called "Capturing 'People of the South Wind,'" saying, "Intention endangers creation."[3]

Going on to assess the power of language to convey abstract ideas, Stafford concludes that communication is interior—not, in his phrase, an "absolute phenomenon." Therefore, he decides to trust the unconscious linkings (he calls them "logicings") that work through combinations of words. "Another way is to let the language itself begin to shape the event taking place by its means."[4] This statement may seem like a refusal to take responsibility for his meanings, but, read carefully, it is an insistence that meaning is discovered *in* language, not manipulated *by* language. To write in this way is to trust the process to reveal the importance of an event, a feeling, a particular word. It is also to be confident that the imagination is more interesting than the analytic mind. "For a writer, it is not the past or present of words that counts, but their futures."[5]

Stafford was unwilling to play by the "rules" because, for him, the rules did not provide a way of participating in art. The participatory aspect of art was what enticed him. He would rather be alive in conversation, trying on new meanings and ideas, discovering the "unfound bonuses," risking and "frisking" at the party, than to miss the party entirely. "Technique used for itself will rot your soul," he said.[6] It is clear that William Stafford's poems employ a variety of technical skills—a strong iambic beat, careful use of rhythm or rhyme, cadence, formal structures—but, for him, these skills are all secondary to the receptivity that might bring something "new." In fact, the extensive use of slant and internal rhyme would indicate that he is exploring new ways to allow sound to manifest itself in the poetic line, and his quirky line breaks immediately demonstrate ways in which individual words can suddenly become important to the overall suggested meaning of the poem. All of these techniques are tools used to a larger end, and the end is not the individual work of art or its meaning; the end is the life of art and *its* meaning. The process of writing allows access to that life; through art the writer discovers just who and what he is: "The more you let yourself be distracted from where you are going, the more you are the person that you are. It's not so much like getting lost as it is like getting found."[7]

It is natural that Stafford's ideas on the teaching of writing centered around this belief, and that his emphasis was on methods that might help the student find the person he is. In "A Witness for Poetry," Stafford made the transition from speaking as a writer to speaking as a teacher:

> One issue, "How the hell do you teach others to write poetry?" can be answered this way. One thing you do with others is try to encourage them, induce them and be company to them when they go ahead and follow the immediacies of experience. You tell them, "Don't be inhibited, don't be cautious, don't be correct; just go headlong into the experience."[8]

This same view was expressed earlier in a widely published and somewhat controversial essay called "Writing the Australian Crawl,"[9] which was interpreted by some educators (and even some writers) as an abandonment of standards. In that essay Stafford compares the process of writing to the process of swimming. He suggests that beginning writers should overcome their fear and reluctance much the way beginning swimmers must learn to trust the water. To do this, they must submit the body to the water and learn that it will hold them up. Language will hold the writer up. Enter it, learn to float. The prescription sounds so easy. And Stafford does make it sound as though language, that voluptuous being, will somehow help produce a fine result. English teachers, worried about syntax and diction and basic punctuation, do not believe it is as easy as he would make it sound. But his critics' interpretation is often superficial. Stafford at no time implies that the results will be good, only that they will be real, and sometimes surprising. They will come from that interior part of the student where imagination, or inventiveness, converges with a felt necessity to communicate. The result will be something that matters to the student. What better raw material for the exterior "rules" of grammar?

Asked the best thing he can do for his students, Stafford replied:

> Be a listener . . . I think just being really alive to what they say, or write. And that there are all sorts of signals, only a very few of which are routine teacher-signals. My own conviction is—conviction is too strong a word, but the hunch I'm operating on at the moment in teaching writing—is that their moves are the important moves, and mine are sort of counter-moves or receiving moves . . . This may seem too vague. And it leads to many vague sessions.[10]

The emphasis on listening comes as no surprise. As experts wrestle with the problem of writing in today's classrooms, on the elementary as well as the college level, more and more of them advocate the methods that Stafford used for over forty years. This does not mean a reduction in standards, but a revaluation of how those standards should be taught. Revision is the natural result of Stafford's way of teaching, but it comes from the student's urgent need to clarify or explore.

Since writing was a way of living, a means, not an end in itself, Stafford saw himself as teaching something that would be an ongoing resource in the life of the student: "You may find yourself in a continuing way of life that is enriched by the practice of art."[11] He also recognized that his goal was difficult—and often misunderstood:

> It was only far along in my teaching and writing—in the last ten years of my teaching, say, when I was deliberately withdrawing to half-time so as to save precious hours for writing—that I began to understand my way as simply incompatible with that of most others. It became apparent that many teachers, for instance, have forgotten how material begins to seek its own form, how a piece of wood, for instance, may like a certain curve when you are carving a gunstock like the one I admired in the corner of our living room, how a phrase when you speak it or write it begins to call up another phrase, or how a word suddenly finds another word that its syllables like to associate with.[12]

Crossing Unmarked Snow, edited posthumously by Paul Merchant and Vincent Wixon, collects a number of later interviews and essays about the art of teaching. "The Experience of Now," a dialogue with students (also captured in part on the videotape "What the River Says"), shows how Stafford readily gave students authority over their own work:

> And so I feel trapped in a society, and in a school system, that persuades individuals that all their activities are goal-oriented towards some goal that doesn't have anything to do with how they feel. In the arts it has to do with how you feel. So you trust what occurs to you. And you've just got to do that. If somebody else doesn't like it that way, you can make it the way they like it if you want to, but it won't be art. See what I mean?[13]

He went on to say:

> But if you're a writer, now I'm not talking about the kind of writer that's trying to flimflam society. If you're Solzhenitsyn, if you're Tolstoy, if you're these people who are art writers, then the research for what you're writing is your whole life. I mean there is one world expert on it—you. And you're right in the center of your life. So it's not a question of whether you can fool someone else if you're an authority or not. It is that for what you're writing, if you're doing it this way, there is no other authority. There is no other authority. That's where it is. . . . [14]

By offering this approach, Stafford made writing a possibility for countless students. Only a few have become published writers, but it can be assumed that each of them has left the classroom with a better feeling of what it is to enter language, and a better sense of who he or she really is. The effect Stafford's approach can have on a genuinely talented writer is exemplified by the comments of a contemporary poet, Linda Pastan:

> Bill Stafford . . . really made me start looking at writing in a different way. It loosened me up a lot. I used to think that a poem had its shape before you even began, and I knew

ahead of time what I wanted to say. I'd come to the blank page with a specific idea. After talking a lot to Bill Stafford and hearing him talk, I really tried to follow a different path so that I wouldn't have any idea where I was going to end when I began—and that was really intoxicating. I mean, you really made discoveries that way—about yourself—and I think it leads to better poetry.[15]

While advocating writing as exploration, Stafford also said, with his special brand of wit, "Ideally for me, poems are nothing special. They are just the language without any mistakes."[16] The subliminal message here is that it is possible to achieve a kind of perfection. If so, it is a perfection that resides in the reader, not the writer.

It is evident that Stafford believed in the capacity of the reader to complete the process. He assumed that the reader would enjoy the same associative play that he responded to as he was writing. In that meeting of minds, what Donald Hall refers to as "one man's inside talking to another man's inside,"[17] there is room for tenuous connections to be made. Stafford asks the rhetorical question, "Can it be that poetry often allows both writer and reader to swing wide on allusion and hint and loose connection, just because only by such recklessness can one reach far out for meanings, with frail helps from language?"[18] By "taking [his] hands off the handlebars,"[19] letting the poem make its own way for a time, he dares to follow its intuitive path. He trusts the poem implicitly; writer and reader will meet in that nebulous space the poem creates. An interview clarified this further:

Kitchen: Is that your idea of the ideal reader—someone who will listen that hard?

Stafford: That's right. Superconductivity in the head is what I'm after. So that whatever comes is met with resilience, with initial acceptance; it doesn't mean that it isn't processed by your former experience and whatever kind of bounce you have in your own head, but it is, in the first instance, welcomed. That's what I try to cultivate in my writing, too. Whatever I start to write, I don't try to be hard on it—I try to welcome it, make it feel at home, see what it's going to say next.[20]

Although Stafford wrote a few comments or articles on other writers (namely Brother Antoninus, Richard Eberhart, Robinson Jeffers, Thomas Hardy) and some short comments on a few of his individual poems, he carefully removed himself from the field of criticism. Stafford seemed unafraid to judge the critics, however. His judgment came from "inside," assessing any given comment to see if it helps or hinders the writer in his chosen task. "I'm afraid of the conditions under which students, for instance, are inducted into the idea of writing . . . that they are made to feel this obligation to be brilliant, to turn out things that are worthy, and that attitude is paralyzing, I think." He went on to say he feared the loss of risk if he followed the prescriptions of the critics:

> The stance that some people take about doing art—which is a rigid stance, which is that it's got to make American Literature more dignified—is destructive to the recklessness or the willingness to be available to the now-ness of experience . . .
> I believe the general public is not well served by critics and artists who make it seem that doing art is not available to human beings, that it is available only to those who are already accomplished. And when you do art you are not already accomplished—you are blundering in all over again . . .
> I feel that the resultant of discussions about writing is that people who aren't in it get a distorted view of what it's like. I don't think that anyone is trying to distort this view, I'm just saying that in always focusing on successful works—the finished product—they don't realize that writers do a lot of dumb things. . . . Writers have wastebaskets.[21]

Shortly before he died, however, Stafford broke with his habit of refusing to be a critic and wrote a review of Carolyn Forché's anthology, *Against Forgetting: Twentieth-Century Poetry of Witness* (Norton, 1993) for the Winter 1993-94 issue of *Hungry Mind Review*. The posthumous appearance of this review meant that it generated considerable interest in the writing community. For all his commitment to a poetry of witness, Stafford exhibited caution, stating that "there are inherent problems in a collection like this. For instance, the individual glimpses that create the distinction of poetry put a strain on the thesis of the book; poems that buckle down to the thesis can hardly attain the shiver of the unexpected that distinguishes lively discourse."[22] He went on to say:

> The labels in the book, the assumptions, and the speed of assessment almost inevitable to a book with a thesis like this one, put a torque on me, snagged my attention, kept me wary of living on the emotional high of atrocity hunger.

His warning was clear: to yoke a poem to an explicit thesis is to espouse a cause, but not to enter literature: "Poetry flourishes by staying alive to alternatives. Irony haunts it."

It has also become clear that Stafford continued to think about the process of revision and the climate of the contemporary writing workshop. *Crossing Unmarked Snow* not only outlines a careful consideration of his "no praise, no blame" stance, but it also contains two previously unpublished "directives." "Workshop Gleanings" is a kind of self- and group-interrogation which forms an implicit agenda for what an ideal workshop might be. "Grooming a Poem After It Happens" could be called a statement on revision—but if so, it is revision based on a series of open-ended and provocative questions. It carefully avoids holding the poem up to any standard but those imposed by its own structures. This is in keeping with a statement made very shortly before he died in an interview with Michael Markee and Vincent Wixon:

> I'm suspicious of the ability of any fallible human being to erect some kind of standard and say, this is it. The realm of possibility is more glorious than that—that would be one way to put it. The closing in on some kind of hierarchy is a function of the limitedness of the judges more than it is the quality of the work. So I like the idea of operating in that playing field where it's not "tennis with the net down," as Frost said. Tennis isn't enough. The net could never be high enough . . . For me writing is invading that area of "What am I missing?" rather than "Does this reach a standard?"[23]

By continually questioning his own practices, Stafford was not only writer and teacher—he was student as well: "I feel like a student all the time. Life is trying to teach me. Emerging experiences are giving me these opportunities."[24] "I think writing is itself educational, exploratory, and worthy of trust while you're doing it."[25] The reader instinctively feels that Stafford is learning as he is going. Thus the poems never seem to preach—or even teach—so much as to come to a natural conclusion. They embody Frost's adage, "No surprise in the writer, no surprise in the reader,"[26] and, in the case of William Stafford, the reader senses the writer's genuine surprise.

Whitman and Yeats spent their poetic careers revising and revising one long "book"—a central vision of the world. Such efforts as Hart Crane's *The Bridge* and William Carlos Williams's *Paterson* are lauded for a similar attempt. If William Stafford's work is viewed as an equally long "book," it too adds up to a vision of the world. His method of revision was one of addition, of coming at the same material from a slightly altered perspective, of chipping away at the edges of things. "I think it would be possible for me at the end of a long conversation in which we all identified our positions very carefully to say that every poem I have ever written is a quiet protest poem."[27]

If this is so, then Stafford's poems negate ideology even as they struggle, moment by moment, with moral choice. In his darkest, coldest poems, he offers us a landscape in which choices are necessary—then exits the poem. The line break between deer and dead is never resolved. A hundred readings of the poem only serve to reveal the quandary in its many facets. A thousand readings of "What the river says, that is what I say" will not elicit what it is he says. Enigmatic to the end, Stafford leaves us to deal with our own moral issues. The isolated individual must negotiate an inner darkness and nothing—certainly no poem—will ease the complicated nature of a justice that "will take us millions of intricate moves."

Of those born in Stafford's generation, the confessionals would emerge to join the American photograph called celebrity. Yet William Stafford's body of work is certainly as important as that of those of his chronological generation—Robert Lowell, John Berryman, Elizabeth Bishop—and those of his poetic generation—Robert Bly, James Wright, Richard Hugo, Donald Hall. His vision is as broad and as all-encompassing as that of Yeats or Whitman. It is as tightly woven and as imaginatively complex as that of Stevens and as sensitive to the inner landscape as Roethke's. The most natural comparison seems to be with Robert Frost. Fred Chappell said that there was "more Frost in him than Zen"[28] and in a commentary on Stafford's death, the poet Roland Flint remarked: "He and his work exemplify the idea that poetry is submissive; the simple surfaces of his poems hide a sidewinder as complicated and subtle as Robert Frost."[29]

More than to any other writer, Stafford's essays referred to Frost—so much so that Frost appears to be his natural predecessor. Yet when someone else made the comparison, Stafford became testy. In an interview with Cynthia Lofsness, he revealed his irritation:

> *Q*: What do you think of Robert Frost? Why do you think he was singled out as THE American poet?
>
> *A:* Well, I can't help thinking that part of Frost's centrality in American life comes from qualities that are not necessarily good, or not necessarily important for poetry. He lived a long time, he showed up well in photographs, and you know, he came from the right part of the country. . . . His reputation just followed the tide of the pioneers and so on. [Pause.]
>
> *Q:* What about his reputation as the wise old New Englander, and the Backwoods Prophet?
>
> *A: [In a sharp tone]* I don't feel he was wise at all, his political advice seemed to me poisonous, and his influence on politics, if he had any, just seems to me feedback of stereotypes. So I don't consider him a seer at all or wise man or prophet or anything like that. But he was a tenacious old guy who wrote some interesting poems.[30]

The reportedly sharp tone is uncharacteristic. So is the expressly judgmental opinion of another poet. What made Stafford drop his usual stance of tolerance and inclusion? Maybe it was the emphasis on THE American poet. Maybe it was the suggestion of wisdom. But this quick response sounds suspiciously like Harold Bloom's concept of the anxiety of influence. If Stafford did not share Frost's politics or even his poetics, then quite possibly he sensed that, deeper than any rivalry, he shared something else with Frost—a darkness, maybe even a coldness—in that realm where poems begin.

When Frost died in 1963, Stafford's first book of poetry was just being published. Together, these two poets span the twentieth century, offering up a poetry seemingly by and for the people. Thought of as quintessentially American—toughly individualistic, democratic, attempting to capture the rhythms of ordinary American speech—each had to remove himself from America in order to become so "American." Frost, disappointed in his country's inability to appreciate his work and his own inability to farm and write successfully, spent three years in England where, in his early forties, his first two books were published. Only then could he return from his self-imposed "exile." Stafford spent four years in "exile" in the CO camps during World War II. Although he was not physically removed from his country, he was intellectually opposed to its policies and was, in every respect, forced to look at the America he loved from the vantage of an outsider. Poets have always felt themselves to be somewhat exiled from the mainstream. But, in the case of Frost and Stafford, the physical removal seemed to provide a stance from which they could view their country—and themselves.

Frost's famous poem, "Stopping by Woods on a Snowy Evening," explores the attraction of darkness, the longing to set aside human responsibility and enter the woods. "The woods are lovely, dark and deep."[31] The poem moves inevitably toward its repetition ("And miles to go before I sleep")—the pull toward death, and the final refutation. Nature remains apart from us, something to be "entered."

Stafford's "Over the Mountains" locates itself not in the particular, but in the general, making this a peculiarly Western poem where space is wide open; the wilderness is omnipresent, is unowned, familiar in its vastness:

> Maybe someone stumbles across that child
> lost weeks ago, now chilled and unconscious but
>   breathing.
> Maybe a friendly wanderer saved the child
> for awhile, but had to go on, and this is the end.

(The world we all came from reaches out; its trees
embrace; its rocks come down ready to cover
us again. Moss clings to the feet and climbs
carefully protecting its own. It wants us back.)

Now people carry the child, warm him;
"Save him," they say. Then he stirs and opens his
    eyes.
He doesn't want what he sees. He closes his eyes.
The slow tide of the forest takes him away.

(This doesn't happen just once; it happens again and
    again,
to the lost, to searchers and parents, to you, to me.)[32]

The poem begins *in* the woods, so to speak. We don't need to "enter" what we are already within. The child has experienced what it is to be part of (as opposed to apart from) something larger, and he chooses to remain "lost." Or, as the poem seems to suggest, maybe the forest saves him. Maybe *our* responsibility is to learn how to *become* lost, to go into the darkness and the depth.

It is possible that Stafford's sharp tone in the interview was the result of uneasiness, that he suspected he and Frost had more in common than he wanted to admit. That their biggest difference was not philosophy, or even politics, but *sensibility*. Confronting Frost's darkness in himself, he opted to explore the deep. So, in spite of the easy voice of both poems, in spite of the attractiveness of each kind of "woods," there are significant differences. Frost's speaker is individualized; Stafford's seems to be speaking from an almost mythical realm. Frost's darkness is life-threatening; Stafford's darkness (and death) is, in many ways, life-affirming. Frost's form works to emphasize the singularity of the experience; Stafford's movement from the semi-specific to the general to the wholly imagined emphasizes what he then overtly states—it happens all the time, to everyone. If there is metaphor here, Frost's is the personal metaphor of what the woods represent to him; Stafford's is the assertion that imagination belongs to us all.

This attitude was articulated in Stafford's opening remarks for the 1992 videotape entitled "The Life of the Poem":

A writer is not someone who has to dream of things to write, but has to figure what to pick out of the current as it goes by. The current happens to everybody; the selection happens to some; the crystalizing of the selection happens to the writer.[33]

As with all truly great writers, Stafford's "generation" extends beyond the limits his own time. With the posthumous selection entitled *The Way It Is*, contemporary readers, scholars, and critics have, at last, a comprehensive picture of the entire body of his work. It cannot begin to contain all the poems, but it certainly brings together all the most important poems and presents them in the context of his ongoing project. Poems that seemed less significant in their original publication gain in stature as they fit seamlessly into a broader picture. And at the heart, there remains the mysterious darkness which Stafford entered again and again in his attempt to write the world. We inherit not only the poems, but the attitude in which they were written: "I must be willingly fallible in order to deserve a place in the realm where miracles happen."[34]

Notes

Introduction

1. Fred Chappell, "Two Views of the Lone Man,"*On William Stafford: The Worth of Local Things*, edited by Tom Andrews (Ann Arbor: University of Michigan Press, 1993), 143.
2. Stafford, *Writing the World* (Baltimore: Alembic Press, 1988), 11.
3. William Stafford, letter to Judith Kitchen, 15 July 1988.
4. Stafford, "Being a Person," *Even in Quiet Places* (Lewiston, ID: Confluence Press, 1996), 89.

Chapter 1

1. William Stafford, *Crossing Unmarked Snow*, edited by Paul Merchant and Vincent Wixon (Ann Arbor: University of Michigan Press, 1998), 103, originally published in *The Ohio Review*, Fall 1993.
2. William Stafford, *You Must Revise Your Life* (Ann Arbor: University of Michigan Press, 1986), 11.
3. *You Must Revise Your Life*, 13.
4. *You Must Revise Your Life*, 19.
5. William Stafford, *Traveling Through the Dark* (New York: Harper, 1962), 75; *Stories That Could Be True: New and Collected Poems* (New York: Harper, 1977), 96-97; *The Way It Is* (St. Paul: Graywolf, 1998), 96.
6. William Stafford, *Down in My Heart* (Columbia, SC: The Bench Press, 1985). Reprinted Corvallis, OR: Oregon State University Press, 1998), 3.
7. *You Must Revise Your Life*, 12.
8. William Carlos Williams, *Paterson* (New York: New Directions, 1958), 9. "Say it! No ideas but in things."
9. *You Must Revise Your Life*, 21.
10. William Stafford, *Writing the Australian Crawl* (Ann Arbor: University of Michigan Press, 1978), 58.
11. *You Must Revise Your Life*, 111.
12. *Writing the Australian Crawl*, 62, 65, 66.
13. *Writing the Australian Crawl*, 3, 12, 27.
14. George Lensing and Ronald Moran, *Four Poets and the Emotive Imagination: Robert Bly, James Wright, Louis Simpson, and William Stafford* (Baton Rouge: Louisiana State University Press, 1976).
15. Peter Stitt, "A Remarkable Diversity," Review of *A Glass Face in the Rain* by William Stafford, *The Georgia Review*, 36.4 (Winter 1982): 913. Reprinted in *On William Stafford: The Worth of Local Things*, edited by Tom Andrews (Ann Arbor: University of Michigan Press, 1993), 63.
16. *Writing the Australian Crawl*, 60.
17. "Homecoming," *The Rescued Year* (New York: Harper, 1966), 13; *Stories That Could Be True*, 115; *The Way It Is*, 107.

18. "The Little Lost Orphans," *Someday, Maybe* (New York: Harper, 1973), 69; *Stories That Could Be True*, 240.
19. "Fictions," *Stories That Could Be True*, 13.
20. "A Survey," *Stories That Could Be True*, 35.
21. "A Course in Creative Writing," *A Glass Face in the Rain* (New York: Harper, 1982), 65; *The Way It Is*, 195.
22. "A Cameo of your Mother," *A Glass Face in the Rain*, 83.
23. "What I'll See That Afternoon," *A Glass Face in the Rain*, 114.
24. "Looking for Gold," *An Oregon Message* (New York: Harper, 1987), 37; *The Way It Is*, 214.
25. *Traveling Through the Dark*, 94; *Stories That Could Be True*, 107; *The Way It Is*, 102.
26. "In Response to a Question," *Traveling Through the Dark*, 33; *Stories That Could Be True*, 76; *The Way It Is*, 86.
27. "Bi-Focal," *Stories That Could Be True*, 48; *The Way It Is*, 72.
28. "In Fog," *Allegiances* (New York: Harper, 1970), 75; *Stories That Could Be True*, 194.
29. *You Must Revise Your Life*, 9, 8.
30. *An Oregon Message*, 72; *The Way It Is*, 221.
31. "Whose Tradition?," *Writing the Australian Crawl*, 81.
32. "Flowers at an Airport," *Allegiances*, 35; *Stories That Could Be True*, 172-73.
33. "Whenever It Is," *Stories That Could Be True*, 22-23.
34. "The Gift," *The Ohio Review* 40 (1988): 26; *The Way It Is*, 165-66.
35. *You Must Revise Your Life*, 62.
36. *Writing the Australian Crawl*, 77.
37. Jonathan Holden, *Style and Authenticity in Postmodern Poetry* (Columbia: University of Missouri Press, 1986), 33-44.
38. "In Dear Detail, By Ideal Light," *Traveling Through the Dark*, 91; *Stories That Could Be True*, 105-6; *The Way It Is*, 100-101.
39. *Writing the Australian Crawl*, 17.
40. *A Glass Face in the Rain*, 46.
41. Stephen Corey, "Lives on Leaves," review of *Things That Happen Where There Aren't Any People*, by William Stafford, *Virginia Quarterly Review* 57 (1981): 735. Reprinted in *On William Stafford: The Worth of Local Things*, edited by Tom Andrews (Ann Arbor: University of Michigan Press, 1993), 60.
42. Sanford Pinsker, *Three Pacific Northwest Poets: William Stafford, Richard Hugo, and David Wagoner* (Boston: Twayne, 1987), 11.
43. Jonathan Holden, *The Mark to Turn* (Lawrence, KS: University Press of Kansas, 1976), 6.
44. Charles Altieri, *Self and Sensibility in Contemporary American Poetry* (Cambridge: Cambridge University Press, 1984), 11.
45. Altieri, 15.
46. Altieri, 14.
47. Richard Hugo, "Problems with Landscapes in Early Stafford Poems," *Kansas Quarterly* 2 (1970), 35. Reprinted in *On William Stafford: The*

Worth of Local Things, edited by Tom Andrews (Ann Arbor: University of Michigan Press, 1993), 113.

48. "The Third Time the World Happens: A Dialogue on Writing Between Richard Hugo and William Stafford," *Northwest Review* 13 (1973): 31-32.

49. "The Title Comes Later," *Stories That Could Be True*, 99.

50. "Judgments," *The Rescued Year*, 14; *Stories That Could Be True*, 118-19; *The Way It Is*, 110.

51. "Willa Cather," *Stories That Could Be True*, 40.

52. "Sometimes, Reading," *The Ohio Review*, Fall 1993. Reprinted in *Crossing Unmarked Snow*, edited by Paul Merchant and Vincent Wixon (Ann Arbor: University of Michigan Press, 1998), 103-4.

53. Stan Sanvel Rubin and Judith Kitchen, "A Conversation with William Stafford," SUNY Brockport, 22 March 1988.

Chapter 2

1. William Stafford, *Down in My Heart* (Columbia, SC: The Bench Press, 1985). Reprinted Corvallis, OR: Oregon State University Press, 1998), 13.

2. *Down in My Heart*, 78.

3. *Down in My Heart*, 70.

4. "What the River Says," Videotape by Vincent Wixon and Michael Markee, Ashland, OR: TTTD Productions, 1989.

5. William Stafford, *Stories That Could Be True* (New York: Harper, 1977), 29-30. Quotations from poems in this chapter are from this collection; page numbers are indicated in parentheses. Also in *The Way It Is*, 60-61. Italic page numbers indicate poems found in *The Way It Is*.

Chapter 3

1. William Stafford, *Stories That Could Be True* (New York: Harper, 1977), 61. Poems in this chapter are quoted from *Stories That Could Be True*; page numbers are given in parentheses. Also in *The Way It Is*, 77. Italic page numbers indicate poems found in *The Way It Is*.

2. Stafford, "Finding What the World Is Trying To Be," *Writing the Australian Crawl* (Ann Arbor, Michigan University Press, 1978), 122.

3. *Writing The Australian Crawl*, 26.

4. Wallace Stevens, "The Emperor of Ice Cream," *The Collected Poems of Wallace Stevens* (New York: Alfred A. Knopf, 1964), 64.

Chapter 4

1. William Stafford, *Stories That Could Be True* (New York: Harper, 1977), 51; *The Rescued Year* (New York: Harper, 1966), 67. Quotations from all poems in the chapter are taken from *Stories That Could Be True*; page numbers are given in parentheses. Also in *The Way It Is*, 74. Italic page numbers indicate poems found in *The Way It Is*.

2. Stafford, *You Must Revise Your Life* (Ann Arbor: University of Michigan Press, 1986), 69.

3. Robert Frost, letter to John T. Bartlett, *Selected Letters of Robert Frost*, edited by Lawrence Thompson (New York: Holt, Rinehart, and Winston, 1972), 113. "Remember that the sentence sound often says more than the words."

4. "Birches," *Robert Frost: Poetry and Prose*, edited by E. C. Lathem and L. Thompson (New York: Holt, Rinehart, 1972), 261.

5. Stafford, *You Must Revise Your Life*, 19.

Chapter 5

1. William Stafford, *Stories That Could Be True* (New York: Harper, 1977), 3. Page numbers of quotations from this volume are given in parentheses. Also in *The Way It Is*, 49. Italic page numbers indicate poems found in *The Way It Is*.

2. Walt Whitman, "Song of Myself," *Leaves of Grass* (New York: Norton, 1973), 88.

3. Stafford, "Smoke," *Smoke's Way* (Port Townsend, WA: Graywolf Press, 1983), 107; *The Way It Is*, 154.

4. Stafford, "Answerers," *Things That Happen Where There Aren't Any People* (Brockport, NY: BOA Editions, 1980), 13. Page numbers of quotations from this book are listed parenthetically.

5. Stan Sanvel Rubin and Judith Kitchen, "A Conversation with William Stafford," SUNY Brockport, 22 March 1988.

Chapter 6

1. William Stafford, *A Glass Face in the Rain* (New York: Harper, 1982). Page numbers of poems in this volume are noted in parentheses. Italic page numbers indicate poems found in *The Way It Is*.

2. Stafford, "Cheat Grass." *Brother Wind* (Rexburg, ID: Honeybrook Press, 1986), 7. Reprinted in *My Name is William Tell* (Lewiston, ID: Confluence Press, 1992), 64.

3. Stafford, *An Oregon Message* (New York: Harper, 1987), 10. Page numbers of quotations from this volume are noted parenthetically. Italic page numbers indicate poems found in *The Way It Is*.

4. Stafford, *Writing the Australian Crawl* (Ann Arbor: University of Michigan Press, 1978), 87.

Chapter 7

1. William Stafford, *Passwords* (New York: Harper, 1991), 7. Page numbers of quotations from this volume are noted parenthetically. Also in*The Way It Is*, 233. Italic page numbers indicate poems found in *The Way It Is*. Revisions of the poem are reprinted in *Crossing Unmarked Snow* (Ann Arbor: University of Michigan Press, 1998), 36-37.

2. Stafford, *My Name is William Tell* (Lewiston, ID: Confluence Press, 1992). Page numbers of quoted material from this volume appear in parentheses. Reprinted in *On William Stafford: The Worth of Local Things*, edited by Tom Andrews (Ann Arbor: University of Michigan Press, 1993), 271.
3. Stan Sanvel Rubin, "A Trail 'One Person Wide'," Flint Hills Literary Festival, Kansas State University, 1997.
4. Stafford, *Even in Quiet Places* (Lewiston, ID: Confluence Press, 1996), 3. Page numbers of quoted material from this volume are listed in parentheses. Italic page numbers indicate poems found in *The Way It Is*.
5. Robert Frost, *The Poetry of Robert Frost: The Collected Poems, Complete and Unabridged*, edited by Edward Connery Lathem (NY: Henry Holt and Company, Owl Books Edition, 1979), 377-79.
6. Stan Sanvel Rubin and Judith Kitchen, "A Conversation with William Stafford," SUNY Brockport, 22 March 1988.
7. William Stafford, *The Way It Is* (St. Paul: Graywolf, 1998), 8-9. Page numbers of quotations from this volume are noted parenthetically.

Chapter 8

1. William Stafford, "Near," *The Rescued Year* (New York: Harper, 1973), 77; *Stories That Could Be True* (New York: Harper, 1977), 145; *The Way It Is*, 118.
2. "In Dear Detail, By Ideal Light," *Traveling Through the Dark*, 91; *Stories That Could Be True*, 106; *The Way It Is*, 101.
3. "Circle of Breath," *Stories That Could Be True*, 32; *The Way It Is*, 62.
4. Patrick Kelly, "Legend and Ritual," *Kansas Quarterly* 2 (1970): 28-31.
5. Stan Sanvel Rubin and Judith Kitchen, "A Conversation with William Stafford," SUNY Brockport, 22 March 1988.
6. "Hide and Go Seek at the Cemetery," *Someday, Maybe*, 24; *Stories That Could Be True*, 215.
7. "A Living," *Someday, Maybe*, 14; *Stories That Could Be True*, 208.
8. "Vespers," *Someday, Maybe*, 86; *Stories That Could Be True*, 248.
9. *Allegiances*, 20; *Stories That Could Be True*, 162.
10. Henri Bergson, "Introduction to Metaphysics," *The Creative Mind* (New York: Philosophical Library, 1946), 211.
11. Jean Follain, "Meanings of Poetry," *A Field Guide to Contemporary Poetry and Poetics*, edited by Stuart Friebert and David Young (New York: Longman, 1980), 86. "This is what Bergson grasped fully, especially when he asserted that poets explain Time better than philosophers."
12. Rubin and Kitchen, "A Conversation with William Stafford," SUNY Brockport, 22 March 1988.
13. Stafford, *You Must Revise Your Life* (Ann Arbor: University of Michigan Press, 1986), 44.
14. Rubin and Kitchen, "A Conversation with William Stafford."
15. *Writing the Australian Crawl*, 117.
16. Rubin and Kitchen, "A Conversation with William Stafford."

17. "Montana Eclogue," *Allegiances*, 28; *Stories That Could Be True*, 166.

18. "In Medias Res," *Traveling Through the Dark*, 12; *Stories That Could Be True*, 61; *The Way It Is*, 78.

19. "A Message from the Wanderer," *Stories That Could Be True*, 9-10; *The Way It Is*, 52.

20. "Stories from Kansas," *Allegiances*, 42; *Stories That Could Be True*, 177; *The Way It Is*, 124.

21. *Someday, Maybe*, 32; *Stories That Could Be True*, 220; *The Way It Is*, 135.

22. *Someday, Maybe*, 52; *Stories That Could Be True*, 231.

23. *Writing the Australian Crawl*, 53-54.

24. "Traveling Through the Dark," *Traveling Through the Dark*, 11; *Stories That Could Be True*, 61; *The Way It Is*, 77.

25. "After That Sound, After That Sight," *Someday, Maybe*, 59; *Stories That Could Be True*, 235.

26. "Ask Me," *Stories That Could Be True*, 19; *The Way It Is*, 56.

27. "Crossing the Desert," *Someday, Maybe*, 58; *Stories That Could Be True*, 234.

28. "Universe Is One Place," *Traveling Through the Dark*, 43; *Stories That Could Be True*, 81; *The Way It Is*, 89.

29. "In the Deep Channel," *Stories That Could Be True*, 31; *The Way It Is*, 62.

30. *Someday, Maybe*, 86; *Stories That Could Be True*, 248-49.

Chapter 9

1. William Stafford, "A Way of Writing," *Writing the Australian Crawl* (Ann Arbor: University of Michigan Press, 1978), 18.

2. *Writing the Australian Crawl*, 57.

3. *Writing the Australian Crawl*, 33.

4. "Some Arguments Against Good Diction," *Writing the Australian Crawl*, 59.

5. *Writing the Australian Crawl*, 59.

6. "Whose Tradition?," *Writing the Australian Crawl*, 78.

7. Stafford, "A Witness for Poetry," *You Must Revise Your Life* (Ann Arbor: University of Michigan Press, 1986), 62.

8. *You Must Revise Your Life*, 62.

9. *Writing the Australian Crawl*, 21-28.

10. "Roving across Fields: A Conversation," *Roving across Fields*, edited by Thom Tammaro (Daleville, IN: Barnwood Press Cooperative, 1983), 22.

11. "Making Best Use of a Workshop," *You Must Revise Your Life*, 103.

12. "William Stafford: 1914-," *You Must Revise Your Life*, 20.

13. Stafford, *Crossing Unmarked Snow* (Ann Arbor: University of Michigan Press, 1998), 17.

14. *Crossing Unmarked Snow*, 19.

15. Stan Sanvel Rubin, "Whatever is at Hand: A Conversation with Linda Pastan," SUNY Brockport, 4 Nov. 1976.

16. "A Witness for Poetry," *You Must Revise Your Life*, 58.

17. Donald Hall, "Goatfoot, Milktongue, Twinbird," *Goatfoot, Milktongue, Twinbird* (Ann Arbor: University of Michigan Press, 1978), 118.
18. "Breathing on a Poem," *You Must Revise Your Life*, 51.
19. "A Witness for Poetry," *You Must Revise Your Life*, 59.
20. Stan Sanvel Rubin and Judith Kitchen, "A Conversation with William Stafford," SUNY Brockport, 22 March 1988.
21. Rubin and Kitchen, "A Conversation with William Stafford."
22. Stafford, "Traveling Through the Dark," review of *Against Forgetting: Twentieth-Century Poetry of Witness*, edited by Carolyn Forché, *Hungry Mind Review* (Winter 1993-94): 25. Reprinted as "The Current of Humanity," *Crossing Unmarked Snow*, 77.
23. *Crossing Unmarked Snow*, 35.
24. Rubin and Kitchen, "A Conversation with William Stafford."
25. "Facing Up to the Job," *You Must Revise Your Life*, 74.
26. "The Figure a Poem Makes," *Robert Frost: Poetry and Prose*, edited by E. C. Lathem and L. Thompson (New York: Holt, Rinehart, 1972), 394.
27. "I Would Like to Mention Aluminum," *Writing the Australian Crawl*, 143.
28. Fred Chappell, "Two Views of the Lone Man," *On William Stafford: The Worth of Local Things*, edited by Tom Andrews (Ann Arbor: University of Michigan Press, 1993), 143.
29. Commentary, *The Oregonian*, August 1993.
30. *Writing the Australian Crawl*, 99.
31. Robert Frost, "Stopping by Woods on a Snowy Evening," *Robert Frost: Poetry and Prose*, 90-91.
32. "Over the Mountains," *The Long Sigh the Wind Makes* (Monmouth, OR: Adrienne Lee Press, 1991); *The Way It Is*, 184.
33. "The Life of the Poem," Videotape. Produced by Vincent Wixon and Michael Markee. Ashland, OR: TTTD Productions, 1992.
34. "Some Notes on Writing," preface to *An Oregon Message* (New York: Harper, 1987), 10.

Bibliography

Works by William Stafford
Poetry

"Winterward." Dissertation. University of Iowa, 1954. Twelve of these poems were subsequently published.

Poems. Portland, OR: Portland Art Museum, 1959.

West of Your City. Los Gatos, CA: Talisman Press, 1960.

Traveling through the Dark. New York: Harper & Row, 1962. Reprinted by Weatherlight Press, Bristol, England, 1997.

The Rescued Year. New York: Harper & Row, 1966.

Eleven Untitled Poems. Mt. Horeb, WI: Perishable Press, 1968.

Weather: Poems. Mt. Horeb, WI: Perishable Press, 1969.

Allegiances. New York: Harper & Row, 1970.

Temporary Facts. Athens, OH: Duane Schneider Press, 1970.

Poems for Tennessee, with Robert Bly and William Matthews. Martin, TN: Tennessee Poetry Press, 1971.

Someday, Maybe. New York: Harper & Row, 1973.

In the Clock of Reason. Victoria, B.C.: Soft Press, 1973.

That Other Alone. Mt. Horeb, WI: Perishable Press, 1973.

Going Places: Poems. Reno, NV: West Coast Poetry Review, 1974.

The Earth. Port Townsend, WA: Graywolf Press, 1974.

North by West, with John Haines. Seattle: Spring Rain Press, 1975.

Braided Apart, with Kim Robert Stafford. Lewiston, ID: Confluence Press, 1976.

Late, Passing Prairie Farm. Northampton, MA: Main Street, Inc., 1976.

Stories That Could Be True: New and Collected Poems. New York: Harper & Row, 1977. London: Harper & Row, 1980.

The Design on the Oriole. Mt. Horeb, WI: Night Heron Press, 1977.

Two About Music. Knotting, Bedfordshire, England: The Sceptre Press, 1978.

All About Light. Athens, OH: Croissant & Co., Croissant Pamphlet No. 9, 1978.

Smoke's Way (chapbook). Port Townsend, WA: Graywolf Press, 1978.

Tuned in Late One Night. Northampton, MA: The Deerfield Press, 1978. Dublin: The Gallery Press, 1978.

Passing a Creche. Seattle: Sea Pen Press, 1978.

Tuft by Puff. Mt. Horeb, WI: Perishable Press, 1978.

The Quiet of the Land. New York: Nadja Press, 1979.

Around You, Your House & A Catechism. Knotting, Bedfordshire, England: The Sceptre Press, 1979.

Things That Happen Where There Aren't Any People. Brockport, NY: BOA Editions, 1980.

Absolution. Knotting, Bedfordshire, England: Martin Booth, 1980.

Passwords. Seattle: Sea Pen Press, 1980.

Wyoming Circuit. Tannersville, NY: Tideline Press, 1980.

Sometimes Like a Legend: Puget Sound Country. Port Townsend, WA: Copper Canyon Press, 1981.

A Glass Face in the Rain: New Poems. New York: Harper & Row, 1982. London: Harper & Row, 1985.

Segues: A Correspondence in Poetry, with Marvin Bell. Boston: David R. Godine, 1983.

Roving Across Fields: A Conversation and Uncollected Poems 1942-1982. Edited by Thom Tammaro. Daleville, IN: Barnwood Press Cooperative, 1983.

Smoke's Way: Poems. Port Townsend, WA: Graywolf Press, 1983.

Stories and Storms and Strangers. Rexburg, ID: Honeybrook Press, 1984.

Listening Deep. Great Barrington, MA: Penmaen Press, Chapbook Series No. 3, 1984.

Wyoming. Bristol, RI: Ampersand Press, Roger Williams College, 1985.

Brother Wind. Rexburg, ID: Honeybrook Press, 1986.

An Oregon Message. New York: Harper & Row, 1987.

You and Some Other Characters. Rexburg, ID: Honeybrook Press, 1987.

Annie-Over (with Marvin Bell), Rexburg, ID: Honeybrook Press, 1988.

Writing the World. Baltimore, MD: Alembic Press, 1988.

A Scripture of Leaves, Elgin, IL: Brethren Press, 1989.

Fin, Feather, Fur. Rexburg, ID: Honeybrook Press, 1989.

Kansas Poems of William Stafford. Edited by Denise Low. Topeka, KS: Woodley Press, 1990.

How to Hold Your Arms When It Rains. Lewiston, ID: Confluence Press, 1990.

Passwords. New York: HarperPerennial, 1991.

The Long Sigh the Wind Makes, Monmouth, OR: Adrienne Lee Press, 1991.

History is Loose Again. Rexburg, ID: Honeybrook Press, 1991.

The Animal That Drank Up Sound (a children's book, illustrated by Debra Frasier). New York: Harcourt, Brace, Jovanovich, 1992.

Seeking the Way (with illuminations by Robert Johnson). Minneapolis: Melia Press, 1992.

My Name is William Tell. Lewiston, ID: Confluence Press, 1992.

Holding Onto the Grass. Rexburg, ID: Honeybrook Press, 1992. Reprinted by
Weatherlight Press, Bristol, England, 1994.

Who Are You Really, Wanderer? Rexburg, ID: Honeybrook Press, 1993.

The Darkness Around Us Is Deep: Selected Poems of William Stafford. Edited
and with an introduction by Robert Bly. New York: HarperPerennial,
1993.

Learning to Live in the World: Earth Poems by William Stafford. New York:
Harcourt, Brace & Company, 1994.

The Methow River Poems. Lewiston, ID: Confluence Press, 1995.

Even In Quiet Places. Lewiston, ID: Confluence Press, 1996.

The Way It Is: New and Selected Poems. Introduction by Naomi Shihab Nye.
St. Paul, MN: Graywolf Press, 1998.

Prose

Down in My Heart (autobiography). Elgin, IL: Brethren Publishing House,
1947. Reprint Columbia, SC: The Bench Press, 1985. Reprint Corvallis,
OR: Oregon State University Press, 1998.

Writing the Australian Crawl: Views on the Writer's Vocation. Ann Arbor:
University of Michigan Press, 1978. This and the following titles are part
of the University of Michigan's Poets on Poetry series. They contain
essays and interviews which were originally published in literary
magazines.

You Must Review Your Life. Ann Arbor: University of Michigan Press, 1986.

Crossing Unmarked Snow: Further Views on the Writer's Vocation, edited by
Paul Merchant and Vincent Wixon. Ann Arbor: University of Michigan
Press, 1998. This posthumous collection is invaluable in that it collects
Stafford's critical assessments of others under one cover and has many
observations on the art of teaching as well as texts from the videotapes
made by TTTD productions.

Videotapes

William Stafford: What the River Says. A video by Vincent Wixon and Michael
Markee, TTTD Productions, Ashland, OR. 29 min. A portrait
documentary with comments by William Stafford, statements by such
poets as Gwendolyn Brooks, Stanley Kunitz, Marvin Bell, Stephen
Spender, Richard Eberhart, Maxine Kumin, Jonathan Holden, and
Henry Taylor. Also contains a viewer's guide featuring an introduction,
the text of seven poems, bibliography, and discussion questions.

William Stafford: The Life of the Poem. A video by Vincent Wixon and Michael
Markee, TTTD Productions, Ashland, OR. 29 min. The video follows
three poems from their inception in the poet's notebook, their
emergence from the journal to a final form, and looks at some of
Stafford's techniques in shaping a poem. Comments by William Stafford
provide insight into the creative process. Also contains a viewer's guide.

William Stafford: The Methow River Poems. A video by Michael Markee, TTTD Productions, Ashland, OR. 11 min. Music by Todd Barton. A reading of six of the poems used as roadside signs along the North Cascade Highway in central Washington. The poems are read by Garrison Keillor, Naomi Shihab Nye, and one by William Stafford. The signs are shown on location in various seasons.

William Stafford and Robert Bly: A Literary Friendship. Directed by Haydn Reiss. Films for Humanities & Sciences, Princeton, NJ. Originally shown on PBS, sponsored by the Witter Bynner Foundation. Bly conducts an informal interview with Stafford in the form of conversation, anecdote, a filmed session of the two men teaching together. Each poet reads several of his own poems.

Selected Comments on Poetry

Comment on the poem "The Farm on the Great Plains," *Poet's Choice*, edited by Paul Engle and Joseph Langland. New York: Dell, 1962. 142-43.

"No Answer to this Day," on Richard Eberhart's "Am I My Neighbor's Keeper?" *The Contemporary Poet as Artist and Critic*, ed. Anthony Ostroff. Boston: Little, Brown, 1964. 153-57.

"Brother Antoninus—The World as a Metaphor," introduction to *The Achievement of Brother Antoninus*. Glenview, IL: Scott, Foresman, 1967. 1-18.

Analysis of "Traveling through the Dark," *Reading Modern Poetry*, edited by Paul Engle and Warren Carrier. Revised edition New York: Scott, Foresman, 1968. 54-56.

"Finding the Language," *Naked Poetry*, edited by Stephen Berg and Robert Mezey. New York: Bobbs-Merrill, 1969. 82-83.

"Ask Me," *Fifty Contemporary Poets: The Creative Process*, edited by Alberta T. Turner. New York: McKay, 1977. 290-95.

Taking Note: From Poets' Notebooks. Edited by Stephen Kuusisto, Deborah Tall, and David Weiss. A special issue of *Seneca Review* (1991): 226-30. Selections from Stafford's notebooks in 1990-91.

"Traveling Through the Dark," review of *Against Forgetting: Twentieth-Century Poetry of Witness*, edited by Carolyn Forché, *Hungry Mind Review* (Winter 1993-94) 25.

Works about William Stafford
Bibliographies

Macmillan, Samuel H. "On William Stafford and His Poems: A Selected Bibliography." *Tennessee Poetry Journal* 2 (1969): 21-22. Primarily a list of early reviews.

Nordstrom, Lars. "A William Stafford Bibliography." *Studia Neophilologica* 59 (1987): 59-63. Primary and secondary; relatively complete, including interviews and symposia, critical articles.

Tammaro, Thom. "A Chronology of Books by William Stafford." *Roving Across Fields: A Conversation and Uncollected Poems*. Daleville, IN: Barnwood Press Cooperative, 1983. 50-51. Primary bibliography.

Books

Andrews, Tom. *On William Stafford: The Worth of Local Things*. Ann Arbor: The University of Michigan Press, 1993. Part of the University of Michigan Press "Under Discussion" series. Andrews collects a wide array of reviews of Stafford's work along with several general essays on Stafford. An overview of critical opinion over the years. The section of essays on particular poems is of particular interest, with commentary by Linda Pastan, Charles Simic, Henry Taylor, David Young, and Tom Andrews, among others. Excellent comprehensive bibliography.

Carpenter, David A. *William Stafford*. Boise State University Western Writers Series, no. 72, 1986. This 51-page pamphlet deals with the life and poems up until the early 1980s.

Holden, Jonathan. *The Mark to Turn: A Reading of William Stafford's Poetry*. Lawrence: University Press of Kansas, 1976. A look at Stafford's first five books, identifying the linking vocabulary that suggests the larger vision behind the work and calling attention to many similarities with the work of Wallace Stevens.

Lensing, George S., and Ronald Moran. *Four Poets and the Emotive Imagination: Robert Bly, James Wright, Louis Simpson, and William Stafford*. Baton Rouge: Louisiana State University Press, 1976. 177-216. A discussion of the mythic element in Stafford's work, looking at the poems as they reflect Indian myths, but also as archetypal poems that explore the tranditional quest or journey.

Pinsker, Sanford. *Three Pacific Northwest Poets*. Boston: Twayne, 1987. 7-55. An examination of images and attitudes in Stafford's work that would place it in the "northwest" tradition; with some highly idiosyncratic readings of the poems.

Stitt, Peter. *The World's Hieroglyphic Beauty: Five American Poets*. Athens: University of Georgia Press, 1985. 57-106. Essay and interview, "William Stafford's Wilderness Quest." A study of the quest motif with a particular focus on the wilderness, where Stafford moves toward a "mystical union with the spiritual realm." An interesting discussion of the manipulation of time. The interview reveals a playful side which reinforces Stitt's observation that Stafford has an affinity with postmodernism.

Selected Articles, Interviews, and Reviews

Andrews, Tom. "'Knowing': Glimpses into Something Ever Larger." *Field* 41 (Fall 1989): 38-40. A discussion of Stafford's attitudes toward criticism and an assessment of "sensibility" as it asserts itself in "Knowing."

Barnes, Dick. *Field* 28 (1983): 27-34. A refutation of critic Bob Perelman's statement that Stafford creates "a persona of the real life self" and commits the "pathetic fallacy."

Bly, Robert. *The Darkness Around Us Is Deep* (HarperPerennial, 1993). For the first volume to appear after Stafford's death, Bly selected ninety-nine poems and wrote an introduction. The order pays no attention to the original context of the poems; they are instead grouped into categories of Bly's choosing. His introduction says that Stafford will be read in the next hundred years "because the subject of restraining aggression is the most important problem we face."

Chappell, Fred. "Two Views of the Lone Man." *Small Farm* 9-10 (Spring-Fall 1979): 52-54. A comparison of Stafford and Robert Bly, looking at the difference between solitude and loneliness.

Dickinson-Brown, Roger. "The Wise, the Dull, the Bewildered: What Happens in William Stafford." *Modern Poetry Studies* 6 (1975): 30-38. Special Stafford issue. Dickinson-Brown finds in Stafford's work a dullness and a complacency of tone, the result of too little content and too frequent publication.

Gitzen, Julian. "The Listener: William Stafford." *Modern Poetry Studies* 11 (1983): 274-86. In an astute examination of "sound" imagery, Gitzen looks at the escape from self-consciousness that allows Stafford to become a listener.

Haines, John. "A Comment on William Stafford's 'A Way of Writing' in *Field* 2." *Field* 3 (1970): 64-66. A response to one of Stafford's essays, noting that Stafford's method of writing allows him to keep a continuing flow of thought, though the risk is a "low power" material.

Heyen, William. "William Stafford's Allegiances." *Modern Poetry Studies* 1 (1970): 307-18. Looking at *Allegiances*, Heyen identifies characteristic themes, sounds, lines, and rhythms in Stafford's work and notes a falling off from the first three books.

Howard, Ben. "Together and Apart." *Poetry* 160, no. 1 (April 1992): 34-44. A review of "Passwords," noting that Stafford's work has deepened over the years. In a book where his "casual tone seems strangely at odds with his outlook," Howard emphasizes what he terms the "life-force."

Hugo, Richard. "The Third Time the World Happens: A Dialogue on Writing Between Richard Hugo and William Stafford." *Northwest Review*

13 (1973): 26-47. William Stafford issue. A wide-ranging discussion of techniques, working methods, perspectives, influences, and a sense of place.

Jackson, Richard. *Acts of Mind: Conversations with Contemporary Poets.* Tuscaloosa: University of Alabama Press, 1983. 126-31. A cohesive interview with comments on form, doubleness, human limitations. Jackson's commentary elucidates how Stafford's work can be seen to demonstrate the basic linguistic theories of Jacques Lacan.

Kelley, Patrick. "Legend and Ritual." *Kansas Quarterly* 2 (1970): 28-31. A discussion of family legend and ritual, including the church, the library, and friendship, and concluding that Oregon serves as an extension of the prairies of Kansas.

Kramer, Lawrence. "In Quiet Language." *Parnassus* 6 (1978): 101-17. Saying of Stafford's poems that "the quiet is their goal," Kramer notes a characteristic sentimentality and a refusal to risk intensity.

Lauber, John. "The World's Guest—William Stafford." *Iowa Review* 5 (1974): 88-100. Lauber looks at Stafford's relationship to the earth, especially in the poems about the American Indians. He also pays special attention to Stafford's use of active verbs.

Lensing, George. "William Stafford, Mythmaker." *Modern Poetry Studies* 6 (1975): 1-17. Special Stafford issue. Lensing examines the shadow image for its symbolic dimensions, discovering a mythology that aligns the surface and subterranean worlds.

Lieberman, Laurence. *Unassigned Frequencies: American Poetry in Review, 1964-77.* Urbana: University of Illinois Press, 1977. Review of *Someday, Maybe.* Calling Stafford's quiet language and taciturn voice a "shock of steadiness," Lieberman discovers what he calls a racial memory and a subtle rigor of thought.

Low, Denise. *Re-Publish* 1 (Spring 1994): 5-6. Published after Stafford's death (he sent some poems on August 25, 1993), this profile includes three poems and a commentary on the poems and Stafford's reputation by Kansas poet Denise Low.

Lynch, Dennis Daley. "Journeys in Search of Oneself: The Metaphor of the Road in William Stafford's *Traveling through the Dark* and *The Rescued Year.*" *Modern Poetry Studies* 7 (1976): 122-31. Lynch explores the image of the road and varieties of the journey motif in Stafford's work: journeys of remembrance, journeys of quest, and journeys of experience.

Miller, Tom P. "'In Dear Detail, By Ideal Light': The Poetry of William Stafford." *Southwest Review* 56 (1971): 341-45. In one of the first essays to note the new sets of meanings to be "sprung" from Stafford's clusters of sound, Miller examines Stafford's informal style for its effect on readers, listeners, and critics.

Nathan, Leonard. "One Vote." *New England Review and Bread Loaf Quarterly* 5 (1983): 521-24. Nathan discusses "At the Bomb Testing Site" as an example of a public (or political) poetry that works, not through rhetoric, but through an effacement of personality.

Simic, Charles. "At the Bomb Testing Site." *Field* 41 (Fall 1989): 8-10. Twelve discrete paragraphs responding to particular lines in Stafford's poem, one Simic describes as "a political poem in which not a single political statement is made."

Wagner, Linda W. "William Stafford's Plain-Style." *Modern Poetry Studies* 6 (1975): 19-30. Special Stafford issue. Wagner suggests many similarities between Stafford and Whitman as she explores sentence rhythm, structure, cadence, tone, and natural imagery.

Young, David. "The Bite of the Muskrat: Judging Contemporary Poetry." *Field: Contemporary Poetry and Poetics* 6 (1972): 77-88. Young's essay includes a comparison of Stafford's "Ceremony" and James Dickey's "The Poisoned Man." He finds in Stafford an authenticity of voice and a self-effacement that creates a plausible fiction.

Young, David. "'1940': Shivers of Summer Wind." *Field* 41 (Fall 1989): 45-52. Young sifts through *An Oregon Message* in order to choose a poem he likes, finally settling on "1940" to examine the "risky game" it plays with time.

Zweig, Paul. "The Raw and the Cooked." *Partisan Review* (1974): 604-12. Reviewing *Someday, Maybe*, Zweig accuses Stafford of a "strained simplicity" and "deliberate naiveté"; Zweig, however, confuses the title, calling it *Sometime Maybe.*

Acknowledgments

The following poems (or parts of poems) were included in *The Way It Is: New & Selected Poems*:

"A Course in Creative Writing," "A Glass Face in the Rain," "A Memorial for My Mother," "A Memorial: Son Bret," "A Message from Space," "A Message from the Wanderer," "A Ritual to Read to Each Other," "Across Kansas," "Allegiances," "An Archival Print," "Ask Me," "At the Bomb Testing Site," "At the Playground," "At This Point on the Page," "Bi-Focal," "Ceremony," "Circle of Breath," "Clash," "Connections," "Earth Dweller," "Emily, This Place and You," "Entering History," "Existences," "Fall Wind," "For a Lost Child," "Found in a Storm," "Homecoming," "Ice-Fishing," "In Dear Detail, by Ideal Light," "*In Medias Res*," "In Response to a Question," "In the Deep Channel," "Judgments," "Lake Chelan," "Late at Night," "Level Light," "Life Work," "Listening," "Living on the Plains," "Looking across the River," "Looking for Gold," "Near," "1940," "Not Very Loud," "One Evening," "One Home," "Our People," "Our Story," "Over the Mountains," "Parentage," "Reading with Little Sister: A Recollection," "Remembering Brother Bob," "Report from a Far Place," "Representing Far Places," "Right to Die," "Run Before Dawn," "School Days," "Serving with Gideon," "Slow News from Our Place," "Smoke," "So Long," "Something That Happens Right Now," "Starting with Little Things," "Stories from Kansas," "The Big House," "The Concealment: Ishi, the Last Wild Indian," "The Day Millicent Found the World," "The Epitaph Ending in And," "The Farm on the Great Plains," "The Gift," "The Little Girl by the Fence at School," "'The Lyf So Short'," "The Rescued Year," "The Size of a Fist," "The Swerve," "The Tillamook Burn," "The Trip," "The Well Rising," "Things I Learned Last Week," Thinking for Berky," "Third Street," "Traveling through the Dark," "Tuned in Late One Night," "Universe Is One Place," "Vacation," "Vita," "Vocation," "Walking West," "We Interrupt to Bring You," "With Kit, Age 7, at the Beach," "With Neighbors One Afternoon," "Witness," "Yellow Cars" copyright © 1998 by the Estate of William Stafford. Reprinted from *The Way It Is: New & Selected Poems* by William Stafford with the permission of Graywolf Press, St. Paul, MN.

I am grateful to the Estate of William Stafford for permission to print all other poems included in the original books from Harper & Row.

Additional Acknowledgments:
"Cheat Grass" is reprinted from *My Name Is William Tell*. Copyright © 1992 by William Stafford.

"Deep Light" is reprinted from *Even in Quiet* Places. Copyright © 1996 by The Estate of William Stafford. Both poems are reprinted with the permission of Confluence Press, Lewis-Clark State College, Lewiston, ID 83501.

"Answerers" appeared in *Things That Happen Where There Aren't Any People*, BOA Editions, Rochester, NY, 1980. Reprinted with permission of BOA Editions and the Estate of William Stafford.

"Writing the World" appeared in *Writing the World*, Alembic Press, Baltimore, MD, 1988.

Index

Note: This index includes material found in the notes but not in the bibliography. The titles of works by authors other than William Stafford himself follow the name of the author.